THE JOY

PAUL HOWARD is a prolific author and journalist. A former Spo[rts] Journalist of the Year, his books include the autobiography *Ce[ltic] Warrior*, which he co-authored with boxer Steve Collins, *The Gaffe[rs,] Mick McCarthy, Roy Keane and the team they built*, the bestselli[ng] account of the relationship between Ireland's former manager and his captain, and *Hostage*, a collection of Ireland's most notorious kidnappings. Paul has also achieved great success as the author of the hugely popular Ross O'Carroll-Kelly series.

THE JOY

Paul Howard

THE O'BRIEN PRESS
DUBLIN

First published in 1996 by The O'Brien Press Ltd,
12 Terenure Road East, Rathgar, Dublin 6, Ireland.
Tel: +353 1 4923333; Fax: +353 1 4922777
E-mail: books@obrien.ie
Website: www.obrien.ie
Reprinted 1996, 1999, 2000, 2001, 2002, 2004, 2005, 2007, 2009.

ISBN: 978-0-86278-491-1

British Library Cataloguing-in-Publication Data
Howard, Paul
The joy : Mountjoy Jail : the shocking, true story of life inside
1. Mountjoy Prison 2. Prisoners - Ireland - Biography
I.Title
365.6'092

10 11 12
09 10 11 12

Typesetting, editing, layout, design: The O'Brien Press Ltd
Printed and bound in the UK by CPI Group Ltd.

'Running to Stand Still', words and music by U2 © Copyright 1987 Blue
Mountain Music Limited, 47 British Grove, London W4. Used by permission of
Music Sales Limited. All rights reserved. International copyright secured.
'Give it a Lash, Jack', reproduced with kind permission of Liam Harrison.

MR
28/1/14

C460353594

For Lesley, for everything

ACKNOWLEDGEMENTS

There are a number of people whose involvement with this book, both directly and indirectly, I would like to acknowledge. A huge debt of gratitude is owed to the man whose story is contained within these covers, and to his family, for sharing with me so much of their time, and so many of their memories, many painful, so that this story could be told. I'd like to thank my mother and father, without whose love and support someone else would have written this book. Thanks to Lesley McGovern for the encouragement, advice and belief which helped me through some difficult days. To my brothers Vincent and Richard for reading through the original manuscript and for being such good friends. To Annie Kehoe, a big influence. To all the staff at the O'Brien Press, especially Frances, a great editor who even let me win some of the arguments. To Dave Hannigan, a quiet man and source of never-ending inspiration and humour.

And to the following people who suffered my obsession with this book with great understanding and, in doing so, proved themselves to be good friends: Paul Wallace, Tim Doyle, Neil Fetherstonhaugh, Lorna Dorsey, Colm Murphy, Fíona Dooley, Barry Conroy, Barry Dooley, Gillian Coffey, Lloyd Mullen, Catherine Heaney, Martin Clancy, Fionnuala McCarthy, Roisin Ingle, Fergus Cassidy, Chris McKevitt, Bill Malone, Bryan Cassidy, Tanya Smyth, David Cleary, Pam Miley, Paul Mahony, Gavin O'Connor, Mark Finnerty, Bernard Mullally, Zac Sloper, Liam Dynan, Joe and all the other Egans, and Kevin Fitzpatrick.

You've got to cry without weeping,
Talk without speaking,
Scream without raising your voice.
You know, I took the poison
From the poison stream,
And I floated out of here.

'Running to Stand Still', U2

INTRODUCTION

It was a late-night call to a radio phone-in programme which inspired me to write this book. "There is no point in sending people to jail in this country," an irate member of the public said. "Sure, Mountjoy is just a holiday camp anyway."

This view of Mountjoy Prison does not accord with the facts as recorded by the prison's visiting committee and the Department of Justice, which show Mountjoy to be an institution where, every year, an average of three people take their own lives; where, it is claimed, 65 percent of the inmates at any given time are using illegal drugs; where prisoners are confined to small and often over-crowded cells for up to sixteen hours of each day; and where bullying and violent beatings are known to occur among prisoners, with the victims usually too frightened to report anything to the prison authorities.

Mountjoy Prison does not match the blueprint of what a modern prison should be. Its structure is Victorian and, in some ways, the regime that operates is just as antiquated. The day begins for the prisoners at 8.15am when their cell doors are unlocked and they are ordered to get up, wash, shave, dress and then slop out. This involves bringing their chamber pots down to the toilets, emptying them and cleaning them out. The practice of slopping out has been abandoned in most modern prisons and, while in-cell sanitation exists in the women's prison, the main prison itself lags behind – though prisoners have access to toilets until 11pm. After slopping out, the prisoners then queue for breakfast which they eat in their cells. There is no communal dining area in Mountjoy.

The cell doors are unlocked again at 9.15am when the prisoners are let out for two hours of recreation or work. In recent times, there has been a lot more of the former than the latter, since the traditional services offered by prisons, such as wood chopping and mailsack sewing, are less in demand. The prison authorities maintain that around half of the prisoners have either work, PE or school to occupy them. However, a report this year by the prison's visiting committee contradicted this figure, saying that 500 of the 600-650 inmates were engaged in "daily idleness". They can play snooker, pool, table tennis or chess instead. Most choose to hang around and talk, either in the yard or the hallways where opportunities for drug trafficking occur.

Lunch is served at 1pm and again is eaten in the cells. From 2pm until 4.30 or 4.40pm, the prisoners are out of their cells for rec/work, they eat tea in their cells and are then allowed two hours of television together until 7.20 or 7.40pm when they have their supper and are locked up until the following morning.

Given this daily schedule, the potential for violence is considerable. One prison worker I spoke to during the course of writing this book told me: "People complain about the drug problem inside Mountjoy. Drugs are the only thing keeping the lid on the prison. Without heroin, we'd have dozens of strung-out addicts walking around here every day and the place would be unmanageable. It would explode."

Official prison policy on drugs – whether heroin, hash or hooch, the illegal drink that has been brewed in the prison for generations – is that they are confiscated at all times. Significant resources are put into trying to stop drugs coming into the prison, says prison Governor John Lonergan.

Until recently, the average heroin addict serving a sentence in Mountjoy was offered little or no assistance in coming off drugs. A basic two-week detoxification programme is now offered, followed by a course of Valium to combat the sleeplessness that goes with withdrawal. Critics say that this is totally insufficient. There is a further, more fundamental problem. Detoxification programmes in general have an enormous failure rate, says the Governor. "The important thing to remember is that addicts have to want to be treated and most don't."

The prison authorities accept the fact that, of the 600-650 prisoners who are in Mountjoy at any one time, approximately 200 are drug users. A report by the prison's visiting committee in May 1996 suggested a much higher figure. About 65 percent of Mountjoy's male population are using illegal drugs, it said, though the Governor disputes these figures.

The public's view of Mountjoy Prison has been limited by the fact that little or nothing has ever been written before about the day-to-day reality of being a prisoner in the jail. What little information exists on Mountjoy comes to us through Department of Justice or visiting committee reports on overcrowding, suicide, drug abuse, etc. I wanted to write a book about life inside from the perspective of the only people who know what living in Mountjoy is really like, the prisoners themselves.

The man whose story is contained in this book was introduced to me by a mutual friend. A reformed heroin addict with HIV, he had spent almost all of his adult life inside. As a teenager, he was first in St Patrick's Institution, the young offenders' institution which is next to the women's prison behind Mountjoy, and then in the main prison itself. St Pat's, he told me, was his primary school, Mountjoy his secondary school. All of the offences for which he was committed to the prison involved robberies to get money to buy drugs.

When we met for the first time, we each laid down a pre-condition. His was that his identity should be hidden. As a result, identifying facts, such as his criminal record, sentence, placenames, and the names of other characters appearing in this book have been altered.

My only pre-condition was that he should tell me the true story of what went on behind Mountjoy's walls during the years he spent there. In doing so, he exploded quite a few myths for me. For instance, the relationship between the prisoners and the staff is not as bad as many might believe. He witnessed little or no brutality from prison officers during his time inside. Nor, he said, is rape a problem.

But for almost a year, I listened to his stories about the decade he spent inside, some of which were hilarious, many of which were harrowing. He told me how he witnessed some savage beatings among prisoners. He told me about methods he and other prisoners used to smuggle drugs into the prison, how he shared needles with prisoners with HIV, how he unsuccessfully attempted to get off drugs, how prisoners he was close to committed suicide, how he made a half-hearted

11

attempt to take his own life as a "cry for help", how he watched prisoners mutilate themselves, how he and other inmates fashioned their own weapons to fight with and how he used his time out on temporary release to commit more crimes. All that he told me was cross-checked with prison staff, prisoners and other sources and I am satisfied that the story presented here is an accurate reflection of his life inside Mountjoy over the ten-year period. It must be remembered, however, that certain aspects of prison life as depicted here have since changed, for example, sex offenders are now separated from the other prisoners to protect them from random attack.

For me, the most striking comment he made during the year we spent talking about the prison came when I asked him about the "revolving door syndrome", the mistaken perception that most prisoners sentenced to Mountjoy come in, serve a tiny fraction of their sentences and are then let out again. "It doesn't matter whether you're serving one week or one year," he told me. "When you're looking at the door from the inside, it doesn't revolve fast enough."

Finally, in reading his story – and before making statements such as "Mountjoy is just a holiday camp"– it is important to bear in mind the following statistics. Official figures show that the prison, which can reasonably accommodate 450 inmates, houses a daily average population of 628. Figures for the number of suicides in Mountjoy are difficult to come by. The official government figures refer simply to "deaths in prisons and places of detention", whether by way of suicide, drug overdose or natural causes. However, in 1995, three prisoners took their own lives and a further thirteen attempted suicide. According to Department of Justice figures, 70 percent of prisoners in Mountjoy re-offend after their release.

This book does not purport to offer a solution or even an alternative to imprisonment as a means of dealing with crime whether related to drug abuse or not. It is simply one man's story, but one which I hope will give the public a true insight into life in Mountjoy.

Paul Howard
May 1996

PUNISHMENT

THE GREAT ESCAPE

I've never been so happy to see a bird. I've never been so excited about seeing a babby either. The way I take it across the table and tenderly touch its cheek, you'd swear I'd seen the fuckin thing before. "Coo-chee coo-chee coo, who de big girl den?" I say, just for effect, like, in that stupid way parents talk to their kids. "You're gettin a big, big girl, aren't you?" The thing could have been twice that size when it was fucking born for all I know or care. I don't have a clue who owns it or how me visitor persuaded them to lend it her. All I know is that as long as that screw, Hawk-eye, keeps his beady little eyes on me, then I'm going to carry on playing the role of the doting father.

"What's the weather like out?" I ask without any enthusiasm at all, me junk apathy making even small-talk a chore.

"Not bad," the bird says, with equal indifference. She knows that I'm so strung out I don't really give a shite whether she walked into The Joy in a snowstorm. The pain that started in the pit of me stomach about half an hour ago is making its way up through the rest of me body. Me bones feel like they're being crushed together in a huge vice grip that's being tightened with every minute that passes. The energy in me body's just draining away.

Hawk-eye's after turning his head, so I slip me finger up the sleeve of the babby's cardigan. There's nothing there. I tug the elastic on the other sleeve and nothing falls out either. I know it has to be in the nappy then. I slip me hand up the thing's skirt and in between the

14

towelling and the plastic cover, thanking fuck that it hasn't pissed itself today, or worse. A quick rummage around and the package drops into me hand. It's quite a big one, even when flattened and wrapped in clingfilm. There must be enough there for seven or eight turn-ons. I grip the package in me fist, pull me hand out from under the babby's skirt and hand the thing back across to the bird. "Getting bigger every time I see her," I tell her. I am the king of glibness.

Now for the difficult bit. In me pocket, there's a bit of jacks roll, onto which I've rubbed some butter. I use it to grease me middle finger and then sit jack-knifed forward in me seat, pretending to be interested in some titbit of information me visitor's giving me about the price of fig-rolls, a car crash in which loads of people died or some other shite. I try me best to listen, but me glazed expression is a giveaway. I couldn't really give a fuck about anything at the moment, except what's in me hand and how I'm going to get it into me body.

The sweat's blinding me and me t-shirt's sapping. I fix the package around me buttered finger, slip me hand down the back of me trousers and into me jocks and then sit back. Relaxing me sphincter muscles allows me to get it up me arse quite effortlessly, the butter helping me slide me finger right the way up and leave the package where the sun doesn't shine. I whip me hand down quickly just as Hawk-eye passes and I continue with the bit of chat across the table. He gives me a filthy look. If he only knew what I'd just shoved up me hole.

It's actually behaving itself up there and the lack of discomfort makes a nice change, I must say. Maybe the walls of me arse are starting to develop a resistance to pain after all this time. I think about the time I watched one of the lads in the visiting room shove a package the size of a black pudding up his back passage without a lubricant and without even bringing tears to his eyes. There's a theory in here that the anal capacity of your average heterosexual, heroin-using

Mountjoy prisoner increases in direct proportion to the acuteness of his addiction. Still, I don't need to know the diameter of me own hole to know how bad me need is. It seems like ages until the visit's over but, when it is, I say a quick goodbye to the bird and babby and brace meself for the search by the screws. To say I'm nervous is the under-statement of the century. Me arse is clenched so tight, you couldn't fit an American Express card between me cheeks. It's no more than the usual search, though, a quick frisk to make sure I haven't slipped an Uzi into the pocket of me jeans.

Back in me cell, there's no need to go rummaging about for the package, 'cos I can feel an auld pony and trap coming on. So I just sit on me piss-pot in the corner and let nature take its course. The pony drops eventually, forcing out me little parcel. I pull it out of the pot and rinse the shite and piss off it with water from the jug on me locker. I move over to me locker, peel off the clingfilm and open out the cigarette paper. There's not quite as much as I reckoned, but there's enough to see me through the weekend anyway.

I switch on the radio and it's Bob Marley and the Wailers' "Satisfy My Soul". What a song. Too fuckin right, Bob. I am happy, all of the time. I sing to the brown powder on the table. A bit of Bob always goes down well. Liked a bit of blow himself, he did. Nesta Robert Marley, musical genius and druggie, this one's for you.

I raise the volume so the screws don't suspect what I'm up to. I open up the drawer of me locker, put me metal spoon in it and then slam it shut, jamming the handle in tightly and leaving the roundy bit sticking out. As delicately as me trembling hands will allow, I tip some of the brown powder onto it and, taking the needle off the end of me works, I draw about five millilitres of water from me jug and squirt it onto it. Me lighter is running short on juice, but there should be enough left to cook up this shot. I run the flame backwards and forwards underneath the spoon, using the prong of a fork to try and stir the water and powder into something I can inject. The particles are slow to dissolve and it's obvious this gear I'm after getting is more Shake 'n' Vac than smack. I curse the bastard who cut it, but carry on heating and stirring.

Some juice, which I've squeezed from an orange, helps purify whatever the fuck it is I have on me spoon. Slowly but surely the grains disappear, which is just as well because the top of me lighter is so hot now I'll have third degree burns on me thumb if I have to heat this shite any more. I break the tip off a cigarette, pull the cotton piece out of the filter and drop it onto the spoon, before blowing on it, sucking the liquid into the barrel of me works and then attaching the spike.

I move over to the corner, out of sight of the door, sit on me piss-pot and roll up me sleeve. Finding a vein isn't a difficulty for me. Other junkies have told me they'd pay anything for wiring like mine. There's a great big bulbous one on the inside of me left arm. Amazing considering the amount of shite I've put into it over the years, though I plan to rest that arm after this shot and inject into me right for a change. No point pushing me luck.

Me spike's blunt and I've lost count of the number of times I've promised to get a new one. Twenty other prisoners must have used this in the six months I've had it. That's the problem, though. Some of these fuckers have been using the point of the needle to stir the stuff when they're cooking up, blunting the fuckin thing. When it's some other cunt's works you're using, you don't care. That's understandable, because when you're strung out you don't look beyond getting the shite into you anyway. But fuck the bastard who blunted me spike. Sticking it in me is gonna hurt. Not sticking it in me would hurt even more, but. Another spasm of pain in me stomach reminds me of that.

I pierce me skin and, before easing the liquid out into me body, I

17

suck some blood back into the works to make sure I've hit the vein. Then I let it go slowly, like a good ride, delaying the end for as long as possible to heighten the pleasure, until I decide to slam the rest of it home. Me lips start quivering. I fall backwards, me head hitting the floor hard. This wave of adrenalin runs right through me. Every sense is having an orgasm. Me body feels like it's hurtling along somewhere. I don't know where. But I'm out of this shit-hole for the night.

◆　◆　◆

THE PUNCHBAG

One shower a week is all you're allowed in here. One shower a week and one new pair of jocks. Or, I should say, one newly-laundered pair of jocks. That has to be unhygienic. If someone ever suggests rioting on this issue, I'll be the first one up on the roof. Three days away from me next change, these ones are already heavily skidmarked.

I'm on me way down to the top cat on our landing to see would he put a word in with the screws about getting us a couple of pair a week when I hear whimpering coming out of Bucko's cell. The lads must be beating the shite out of him. Me sick sense of curiosity gets the better of me and I tiptoe up to his door. Peering through the crack, I can just make out the shadows on the wall. I can hear loud voices and swearing, punctuated by these painful groans. I put me foot against the door to push it open a bit more, but I press too hard and it swings open. No-one notices, though. They're enjoying themselves too much.

Bucko's arms and legs are bound and he's suspended upside down from the ceiling. Four of the lads are burying punches into him, like boxers hitting a heavy bag, while he swings backwards and forwards and around in circles on the rope, just helpless. One of the lads starts kicking him in the face, which quickly turns into a mask of deep red. Bucko keeps wriggling around like a fish on a line, trying to avoid the punches and kicks, but they're coming at him from all angles now. Too sore and too tired to continue the struggle, his body just goes limp and he hangs there like an animal in an abattoir, waiting for the end, probably preferring it to any more of this pain.

I know all four of these lads, but I don't recognise them today. It's like they're part of a lynch mob or something. The place is beginning to look like a fuckin butcher's shop. One of the lads, who works out a lot and fancies himself as a bit of a Tyson figure, has completely lost the run of himself. He's throwing digs at the rate of two or three a second, and giving a running commentary, Harry Carpenter style. At one point, he slips in a puddle of blood, but gets his footing again and gives Bucko this spiteful look, as though the poor bastard had bled there on purpose just to make him fall on his arse and look stupid. He calls him all the cunts under the sun and then starts beating him so hard I think he's killed him.

The lads look wrecked, like they've just finished a marathon or somethin. Bucko isn't dead. His eyes flicker, showing some vague signs of life and, as he hangs there, I can hear him faintly gasping for air. His breathing's all wheezy, like. Then one of the lads produces a blade from his pocket. I don't want to watch, but me body refuses to move. He walks over to him and tears off Bucko's shirt, the buttons bursting off and flying across the floor. He steadies him on the rope and holds the blade to Bucko's bare back. His eyes are fucking wild. And then he cuts him. From where I'm standing, it looks like he's opened him up from the base of his spine right down to his neck.

Bucko squeals like a stuck pig and he bleeds like one too. The lads stand around to admire their handiwork. Just a few moments, that's all the whole thing takes. I step backwards and run away. I don't know what they plan to leave of him for the screws to find, but I've already seen enough.

◆   ◆   ◆

WE SHALL OVERCOME

I can feel a beauty coming on. Me guts are in rag order. It's the hooch that does it to you, corrodes away your innards. I whip down me trousers as I make a run for the piss-pot in the corner, sit on it and let it all go. The sound is like the noise a washing-up liquid bottle makes when the last drops are being squeezed out of it. I sit there for ages, dropping piece after piece, with the coldness of the pot sending shivers up me spine. After about twenty minutes or so, when I start to feel like I've crapped out half me organs as well, I stand up to have a look at me work. It's kind of tan to yellow in colour, though it's not quite as watery as it felt coming out. There's tons of it, though. The more the merrier as far as I'm concerned, because I'm doing this for The Cause.

The dirty protest in The Joy is into its third day, with the Governor still showing no signs of shifting on our demand to be let out of our cells to the jacks if we want a pony in the middle of the night. It's inhumane to expect me to sleep in me cell tonight with this kind of stench coming from me piss-pot. Rules are rules, they keep reminding us. Once we're banged up at half-seven at night, there's no getting out until eight o'clock or so the following morning. So we're trying to change their minds. I tear off six or seven sheets of jacks roll in a long strip and fold them up, making sure it's thick enough so as not to let the shit soak through onto me hand. I pull out a nice moist piece, open out the window and drop it to the ground below. I can see at least a dozen other lads doing the same and there are already about a hundred little piles all over the yard. I go back for more, collecting a longer piece this time, which splatters onto the ground below like a lump of cold custard.

Already, the smell outside is overwhelming. It takes me about ten minutes to drop the entire contents of the pot out the window and, as I let go of the final lump, I can see Skidmark opening up his window. Skidmark has the foulest rear-end any of us has ever smelt and that's saying something considering that we're entitled to only one change of jocks a week. I'd hate to have to pick up whatever little surprises he's throwing out.

Not that the Governor will have any difficulty finding someone to oblige. The Bomb Squad, three knackers with a wheelbarrow, a shovel and a brush, will be around at the crack of dawn cleaning the shite up in return for a bit of tobacco. The fumes are powerful enough to knock you out, but these lads seem to be able to stomach it. Yesterday, they collected two wheelbarrows full of the stuff. All for a bit of burn. No amount of gold, never mind burn, could persuade me to clean up the shit of another man. I've got me principles. We've all got our principles. No man should be denied a good shite, even if it is in the middle of the night. I go back to bed and back to sleep, looking forward to eating a hearty breakfast in the morning, so I'll have something to fuck out the window again tomorrow night.

♦ ♦ ♦

In Vino Veritas

Leaving Redser in charge of the storeroom was a bit like having a pit-bull terrier babysit your two year old, if you know what I mean. Redser was a good bloke, though, who grew up and served his apprenticeship in petty crime in and around the same area as me, though we were only ever really on nodding terms as young fellas. This day, for whatever reason, he decided to confide something to me.

"You wanna see what I'm after finding down the stores," he said, sticking his head around me cell door. I looked up from me newspaper. "Wine," he said. "Loads of it."

"Wine?" I asked, me mind racing as fast as his. "What's that doin in the stores?"

"It's altar wine. There's six bleedin bottles of the stuff."

"For the chapel?"

"Yeh ... Listen, what's it like? I mean, could you get pissed on it, could ye?"

"Well, there's definitely alcohol in it," I said, remembering some story I heard about a bunch of altar boys who were knocking it back in the vestry and were pissed at Mass.

"Thinking of robbing a couple of bottles of it today."

"Would you throw us out one?" I asked him.

"Yeh, no problem, man ... I'm still not sure if you'd get locked on it, though."

"Listen," I said, "after a couple of years in here without any gargle, you'd get pissed on a barman's fart."

He laughed on his way out. A couple of minutes later, he returned. "Shit. How am I gonna get it past security?"

That was a problem. The screws were so paranoid about things like razor-blades and forks going missing from the stores, they searched everyone who worked there. I had a brainwave, though.

"Why don't you give it to the Bomb Squad? They'd bring it in for ye, for a bit of burn or something."

"Jaysus, that's not a bad idea."

"But Redser," I called him back as he turned to leave again, "tell them not to go putting the bottles in the fuckin wheelbarrow, under all those shit parcels."

"Come on, I know that, for Jaysus sakes."

"By the way, who's working with ye over there today?"

"Den," he said.

Bollix. Den was a sound enough fella. But he was murder for the hooch, the gargle we brewed ourselves, and I knew if he found out about the wine I'd have no chance of seeing a bottle. "Don't say a word to Den about it," I said to Redser. "You know what he's like. He'd rob the lot for himself."

"I won't. I won't breathe a word, man."

Redser was late back. I didn't know what was keeping him, so I invented some excuse about needing some new soap to get out of me cell and downstairs to wait for him. From the second I saw him coming through the gate back on to the wing, I knew he was gargled. He couldn't walk straight. It was like his legs had a mind of their own. One looked about four inches shorter than the other. He had this stupid smile on his face and he kept on asking everyone were they all right. I don't know how he got through the security gate, but he did and when he saw me he greeted me like a bleedin long-lost brother or something. "Great to see you, ye cunt," he said. His eyes were fucked and he was slurring his words. "Ah wonderful, man, wonderful. Fuggin wonderful. You're a great guy, man. One of the best. One o' the fuggin best. Tellin ye."

One of the screws was doing his rounds, looking for the slightest breaches of prison rules to put you on report or get you banged up in

23

the pad for the night. The other prisoners were being let out for their tea, so I knew I had to get Redser to his cell rapid. "Listen to me," I told him, "I'll go and get your tea, right? I'll bring it up to your cell for you. But you go on up to your peter, do ye hear me?"

"Nah," he hissed at me, "I'll get me tea me–meself."

"Look, you can't walk around in that state. They'll suss you like a light. You'll lose your job as well."

"Ah sure, I'm gonna fuggin lose me job ... anny way," he said. He threw his arm around me shoulder and then whispered loudly into me ear. "I'm after drinking all the wine, man. Me and Den."

"Ye fuckin eejit, ye. I told you not to say nothin to him about it."

"I know, I know. But he sussed me, man. When I was up the step-ladder, getting the stuff down. So we fuggin drank it."

"All of it?" I couldn't believe it. Six bottles. Mind you, he looked drunk enough.

He smiled at me, his eyes only half-open now. "Every last fuggin drop," he said. "Six bottles b–b–b'tween us. Whole fuggin lot's gone, man. We're fugged, so we are."

I wondered about the state of his liver after three bottles of altar wine, would it be just pickled or glowing like a fucking apparition. I put me arm around his waist and walked with him up to his cell, him wobbling all over the gaff and me doing me best not to look like a man helping a drunk up two flights of stairs.

Now, Redser always had a cell to himself and he enjoyed being on his tod. That's just the way he liked it. But even in his polluted state, he knew what was happening the second we got to his landing and he saw two mattresses leaning up against the wall outside his cell. He was off like a bleedin greyhound out of a trap, his anger getting the better of the calming effect of the three bottles of wine. By the time I caught up with him, he was screaming his head off at these two trav-eller lads, who were being moved into his cell. The poor blokes were

24

trying to explain as diplomatically as they could that the caravan –
our name for the cells where the travellers were kept – was full and
the screws had told them to move in with him.

"He told the two of youse to move in?" I asked one of them.

"No," the guy said, "the four of us, boss."

I looked in – there were already two extra bunks inside, as well as
the mattresses the two boys were trying to bring in.

"Well, you're fuggin not moving in here," Redser shouted. "Yiz
can get the fuck out now, so yiz can." He turned to me then: "Can ye
fuggin believe it, man? Wanna put four knackers in me fuggin cell.
Can ye believe the fuggin cheek of it, man? Can ye believe it?"

He worked himself up into a rage, disappeared into the cell and
then came back out dragging the two mattresses behind him. He
picked them up and threw them out on the landing. "I'll give yiz five
men to a fuggin cell, yiz cunts."

The two lads were staying cool, but, which was amazing under the
circumstances. "Listen, boss," one of them said, "it's not our fault.
We'd rather be over with our own kind. But we were told to come over
here."

The two other guests duly arrived with their blankets and pillows.
They saw their mattresses thrown out on the landing and started
exchanging a bit of rapid-fire patter, which me and Redser didn't
understand. It's like they have their own bleedin language or something, those knackers. I reckoned the upshot of it, though, was that
we were going to get battered. One of the four, a huge guy who
seemed to be the boss-man, asked, "What's the problem here, boys?"

Redser, who was too gargled to have any kind of feel for the guy's
tolerance level, just marched up to him, pushed his face right up close
and started shouting: "I've nothing against knackers, right? Live
and let live, that's my fuggin motto. But I went to work this morning
and I left me cell spotless fuggin clean. And when I came back they

were moving four of yiz in. I like being on me own, right? I keep an eye on me cell. If it's fuggin dirty, it's down to me. It's not 'cos yiz are fuggin knackers or an'thin like that. It's just I can't live in a fuggin cell with four fuggin other blokes, ye know?"

I had me arm on his shoulder, trying to calm him down, when a screw who had heard the commotion suddenly arrived up. Redser lit into him. "I hope you heard all that, did ye? 'Cos that's it, no-one's stayin in here wi' me. Four other blokes in me cell? Are ye fuggin mad or wha'? An anyway, it's not just that either. If the caravan's over-crowded, then that's no-one's fault but your fuggin own, right? So when the prison is over-fuggin-crowded, youse have to let fuggin people out. So by movin them in here, that means you're stoppin four," he held up four fingers for effect, "four fuggin people ... four fuggin people from gettin out."

The screw went off and I grabbed Redser's arm tightly. "Will ye relax. You keep that up and they're gonna know you're gargled. The last thing you should be doin is drawin attention to yourself."

He looked at me, this vacant expression on his face. The guy was so locked, it was as though he'd forgotten who I was.

"Tell you what," I told him, "I'll go down and get you a nice cup of tea and we'll talk about this, right?"

I went down and stood in the queue, two teapots on me tray, trying to think up some excuse for collecting the fucker's tea for him. "He's feeling a bit sick," I told the screw in charge.

"Sick?" he said. "That's funny, he was fucking buckled last time I saw him."

There was no point in lying to him. Sure, it was obvious to anyone with two eyes in their head that he was out of his bin. "Tell him to cop onto himself," he said as I went back up the stairs again. "He's a lucky man. You should have seen the state of Den. They brought him straight down to the strip cell to sleep it off. Out of his tree, he was. So tell yer mate to keep his head down."

No chance of that happening. By the time I got back up to the landing, Redser'd passed the point of no return. The knackers were all standing outside, arguing and shouting among themselves, their blankets and pillows thrown on the ground beside their mattresses and the cell door shut tight. "He's gone mad," the boss-man said to me. "He's a lunatic. A madman ... He's barricaded himself in."

The bases of the five beds had been shoved up against the door and Redser said he was staying there until all this five-to-a-cell shite was over. In his cell, there was an old broom cupboard where they used to keep the mops and cleaning equipment, which stank so badly they had to knock a couple of bricks out of the wall to air the place out. Through this hole I was able to speak in to him, to try to talk him round like. "Redser, the screws will break this wall down in a second. Then what are ye gonna do?"

"I don't give a bollix if they put me in the pad," he said. He was talking in a real spoilt child's voice.

"Den's already in there," I told him.

He started laughing. "I told him he'd get caught. Can't hold his fuggin drink, that f-f-fella."

"You're as bad as he is, ye fuckin eejit, ye. Why don't you come out before the screws come up?"

"I'm going down to see the acting chief officer," he said.

"How can ye? You're barricaded in, man."

"Oh yeh. Well listen, right? You get him and I'll talk to him through the hole then. I only want me rights, that's all. That's what I'm doin this for."

The ACO arrived up and was reasonable enough. "We can work this out, but you have to open the door first," he told Redser through the hole.

"I'm not opening no doors till I get me demands."

27

"Well, what are your demands?"

Redser had to think for a bit. "Right, I want yiz to either leave me in here on me own or to let the knackers in and move me to a one or two man cell right now. None of this five-to-a-cell shite."

"I can't promise you anything, you know that."

"Right!" Redser shouted. "I can't promise you when I'm coming out. I'm going on hunger-strike."

The ACO threw his eyes up in the air. Then he looked at me. "He seems to be very matey with you. Can you talk him round?"

"I hardly even know the fella," I said. "I can't tell him what to do. And anyway, I don't blame him. He's only looking for his rights, so he is."

The guy just shook his head. "Looking for his rights? Who does he think he is, Bobby Sands?"

He went off then and I called Redser back over to the hole. "What's the story with all this hunger-strike shite?"

"Not shite," he said. "I'm going on a hunger-strike to get me demands."

"Are you sure you can go through with it?"

"Fuggin right I can ... Got any Mars bars on ye, have ye?"

"What for?"

"Case I get hungry in the middle of the night."

"Redser, you're supposed to be on hunger-strike, man."

"Yeh, that's the thing about hunger-striking, ye know, it gives you a ferocious appetite. Fug me, I'm starvin already ... Anyway, doesn't matter if you eat, so long as they think you're on hunger-strike."

"Yeh, whatever you say, Redser."

"Hang on," he said, "they might block up this hole to stop people talking to me. Will you go around and see what munchies you can get me, so at least they can't starve me out, right?"

I felt like a bit of a prick going from cell to cell, asking for cakes, biscuits and bars of chocolate in aid of Redser's hunger-strike. But most of the guys were generous. The hungry bastard sat on the floor, with his back to the wall, eating his way through everything. Passing his cell, all you could hear was this munching noise. I was standing outside, wondering to meself how much mileage Frank Carson could get out of a Mountjoy "hunger-strike" joke, when the Mountjoy riot squad, or "the kickers" as we called them, arrived. I made one last effort to try to talk him into giving himself up, but he was too stubborn.

A jack was set up on the landing and, within a matter of seconds, a hole had been blown in the wall and the kickers were all over him, dragging him out. "I want me fuggin rights," he was shouting. The hunger-strike was over after an hour and a half, with Redser emerging, I'd say, a few pound heavier than when it had begun. They dragged him down the stairs and into the pad – the cooling room for bad boys. Redser, though, had been a very, very bad boy, so he was probably gonna lose some of his remission on top of that.

That was last night. Redser. The hard man. The rebel. A fighter to the end. I can't wait to see him to tell him the news that he's going to be me new cell-mate. This could be the start of a beautiful friendship.

♦ ♦ ♦

FOR THE BIRDS

Mad Frankie's nickname undersells him. He's not just mad. He's one sick fucker. I'm looking out me window across at him right now and I can see what he's at. He's dangling the little slab of butter he got with his lunch out the window on a piece of twine, trying to attract a seagull. Hidden in the butter is a blade which Frankie's removed from his razor and broken up into pieces of shrapnel, the mad bastard's favourite weapon in his campaign to cull Dublin's seagull population from the comfort of his prison cell.

Sometimes he'll spend half an hour or more waiting for a bite. He'll swing the piece of butter backwards and forwards, then in circles, then tug it up and down on the twine, trying to get the sun to shine on the gold wrapping and create a glare that will catch the eye of a passing bird. He doesn't have long to wait today. One arrives within a couple of minutes and starts to tug at the little parcel.

Not content with just killing the bleedin thing, Mad Frankie plays a little game of tug-o'-war to make the bird more and more desperate to get at the parcel. It's as though he gets some kind of sexual kick from the fact that the gull is not only going to die, but is helping itself to be killed. He leers at the creature before eventually releasing his grip on the twine and the bird flies off with the butter in its beak. As I watch him, I count: "One, Two, Three, Four, Five."

The bird's wings seem to be getting heavier, their movement less frequent. Then it drops to the ground like an apple from a tree. Barely made it out of the grounds of the prison and there it is. Dead. I'm not real fond of animals, like, but the poor thing was doing no harm to no-one. It was just out there, doing its own thing, winging it up and down the coast all day, catching the odd fish. An honest day's pay for an honest day's work. It just had the misfortune to come in from sea and happen on this big menagerie of fucked-up people.

Mad Frankie shows no signs of pleasure after seeing the bird fall out of the sky, which is what's most disturbing. If he got a laugh out of it at least you could say he was just an evil bastard. But this real serious look on his face as he watches the creature die makes me think there's something sick, something mental, going on in his head. There'll be no bragging about this later on. He won't mention it to anyone. He doesn't kill seagulls to bolster his reputation as a bit of a headcase. He does it for his own perverted self-gratification. That's what's so scary about him. Mad Frankie is one sick fucker.

◆　◆　◆

CARL

I can't make out whether the room is spinning or just me bed. Me body feels damp and cold and I pull the duvet tight around me chin. Slowly, I force me eyes open and discover, with a bit of a start, that Tina Turner is standing at the end of me bed with her legs a mile apart and the leather wristband that she's wearing as a skirt up around her ears. Tina, what are you doing here? She doesn't say anything. She just stands there, with her lips pouted and her eyes trained on me, seeming to say, "I want you. I want your dick." Tina. Tina, I love you. I always have. I promise I'll never treat you like that auld bollix Ike did, if we just run away together now. Tina, make love to me. Let's ...

Shite. I'm after puking in me sleep. It's thick, like porridge and all over me chest, me duvet and me pillow. The smell makes me retch, but I've fuck-all left in me stomach and it hurts me. Jaysus, I'm marinating in me own vomit here. Me mind is starting to come to life again and I'm thinking about what happened last night. Our landing had been brewing a barrel of hooch for about a month. We hid a big drum in the store where they keep all the cleaning gear. We filled it up with water, dropped in a few apples and oranges and some yeast which we robbed from the bakery and then stirred it every day. Yesterday, we decided it was ready. I shouldn't have drunk so much of it, though, not when I had a turn-on for later as well.

Me turn-on. Fuck, I've just remembered ... I pull me hand from under the duvet and feel around the floor, eventually putting me hand on me works and me spoon. I slip them under me pillow, which looks like it's been steeped in a bucket of puke overnight. Finding the rest of the incriminating evidence takes more of a thorough search. I roll out of the bed and crawl over to the corner, where I can see me bit of filter and the paper the turn-on came in. I roll them up into a ball and fuck them out the window.

I take a long look at meself in the mirror. I look tired and fucking malnourished, man. Pale and gaunt and drawn, like I've seen me friends look in the past. But never meself. Maybe I did, but never noticed. I don't know. I couldn't give a fuck anyway. While the puke on me bedclothes is still wet, the bit I vomited all over me chest has turned crusty. I pour some water from me jug on to me hand and and start to rub it off, me whole body tightening up as I feel the ice-cold water on me skin. It takes a good five minutes of rubbing to get the stubborn bits off and when I'm finished I turn the duvet and pillow over and slide back under the covers. I'm shivering with the cold.

Tina's still looking at me. A poster of one of the most fanciable women in the whole world adorning a wall that had been dull and lifeless for so long. Fair play to ye, Tina, you don't look eighty years of age, or however old you are. The culchie I kidnapped her from must be pissed off this morning, looking at his blank wall, but sure these are the perks of being put on painting duties. It was a few years since I was on a painting party. In fact, the last time was when I was back in the borstal. It was the time, I remember, that we were all holding out against plans to plaster and paint our landing. It was known as Coronation Street because it was the only one of the eight which still had the old red and brown bricked walls. Most of the lads were from either Fatima Mansions, Dolphin's Barn, the Oliver Bond, Bridgefoot Street or Cook Street. The walls reminded everyone of home and they were allowed to keep them bare as our own personal tribute to the Corporation's foresight in building flat complexes for working class people in the inner city.

Anyhow, back in the borstal, I had been offered this job on the painting party that was decorating one of the other landings and I'm fucked if I can remember even opening one tin of paint for the whole week. I do remember playing a lot of poker, smoking meself blind and tearing down posters, to paint the walls behind them – well, really to get a bit of decent wanking material for me own cell. In the days before heroin became the only currency of real value in The Joy, a Samantha Fox or Linda Lusardi picture could buy you practically anything. I remember getting fifty smokes off a bloke for a Bonnie Tyler promo picture for "It's a Heartache" and I can also remember a Charlie's Angels poster I wouldn't part with for anything, because I thought Farrah Fawcett Majors, Kate Jackson and Jaclyn Smith were the biggest rides I'd ever laid eyes on.

I'm woken up from me little daydream by the sound of me door being unlocked and pushed open. "Morning, morning, morning!" the screw's shouting. "Rise and shine. Up you get. Make your bed and slop out."

I struggle to me feet, grab me piss-pot and walk out onto the landing. The first sight to greet me is Carl's furniture, which has been removed from his cell and stacked neatly on the landing. He must have been shanghaied out or something. All the boys are on top of his stuff like fucking vultures descending on a carcass, claiming his shelf unit, his chair and everything else that's worth taking for ourselves.

"Where the fuck do you reckon Carl's gone?" I ask one of the boys. He just shrugs his shoulders and carries on rooting. Fuckin mystery that. I thought he'd a while left to serve. Last I heard he'd gone off to get tested for some fuckin virus or something that queers get. But sure, he's not queer. I know that for a fact.

Then one of the lads, Casso it is, comes up behind us and screams, "Leave that fuckin stuff alone, youse eejits!"

I nearly shit meself.

"It's contaminated," he says.

We all look at each other. "Contaminated?"

He nods his head. "Contaminated. So don't touch any of it. You'll catch Aids."

◆　　◆　　◆

TALL STORIES

Johnny is at it again. "Met this bird, right? And we're sitting in the station, watching this bloke walking up and down with a briefcase. I says to her: 'Keep an eye on yer man, I'm gonna touch for his case.' So I wait for me moment, right? And then I decide it's time to strike. But just as I'm about to get up, I see another bloke and he's got a case as well and he's looking a bit shifty. I says to the bird: 'There's a switch going down here.' And then ... *BANG*. I see him change the case and I know it's either gear or money. So I says to meself, right, I'm goin for it."

He does me bleedin head in at times. Johnny's criminal record consists of nothing more serious than dipping pockets, but he has this ability to make a shoplifting expedition sound like a multi-million pound bullion heist. As well as that, he's always bragging about his heroin addiction, even though everyone knows the cunt's nothing more than a labour day junkie who spends a tenner on gear when he gets his dole and always tries to persuade someone else to get stoned with him. That's what sets the casual user apart from the real junkie who doesn't give a fuck if anyone else scores. He's a bare-faced fucking liar and the one he's treating the lads to at the moment is one of his personal favourites from the *Johnny the Spoofer's Pocket Book of Telling Pork Pies to Win Friends*.

What's most worrying is that, while me and most of the other blokes in here know that this sting he's talking about was really nothing more than a handbag snatch, some of the more gullible lads and the new arrivals are lapping it up. They're all sitting around him, smiling and shaking their heads in admiration, like a bunch of fucking knicker-wetting schoolgirls fawning over a rock star. He indulges himself a bit more: "So I says to the bird: 'Right, you go over, drop your coat on the case, like it's an accident, pick it up with the case under it and leg it to the door. When yer man tries to follow you out, I'll put the block on him, you leg it up the road, hop into a Jo Maxi and I'll meet you later on.'"

I'm reminded of the times I used to bump into him when we were both living rough in London. Once, I crashed in this shop doorway up at Charing Cross after a party and woke up at about six o'clock in the morning, freezin me arse off. I caught a tube to Euston, where I spotted Johnny sitting on a bench outside the men's jacks. Tube stations were such a favourite hangout of his, I always suspected he was on the game and this day I was bombed out of me head enough to ask the fucker out straight: "Johnny, what's the story, are you a rent boy or what?"

He gave me one of his famous wounded looks. "What the fuck do you think I am?" he said. Real hurt, like. "A rent boy. Jaysus sakes. I'm a fucking stroker, man. A villain. When I need money, I just hatch a little scheme. That's me talent, man. Spottin openings and capitalising on them. I don't have to sell me arse to get dosh."

"Sorry, Johnny. I thought ..."

"That's all right. It just so happens that you've arrived at the right moment, me auld segosha. There's rich pickings to be had here, you know. Oh yeh."

He looked around and then whispered into me ear, "There's something going down, you know."

"What do you mean?" I asked, not realising that I was only encouraging the fucker.

"I'm after been sitting here for half the night, right? A bloke went into the jacks there two hours ago with a brown briefcase and he hasn't come out yet."

"Maybe he's after having a heart attack and died on the floor or something," I said.

"No, no, I went in a few times to suss it out and he's still in one of the cubicles. I looked under the crack at the end of the door and I could see his feet and I could hear him rattling paper around. I reckon he's counting out money. As soon as he comes out, I'm going to touch for his case."

Over the next few weeks, Johnny and me enjoyed many of these conversations on many benches outside many tube station toilets. But because he never seemed to flash any of the sponds he claimed to have earned from his various "jobs" and "blags" and because he slept in shop doorways and signed on the labour every week, I began to suspect that he wasn't quite the master criminal he claimed to be. But he'd still spend entire days, usually at King's Cross or Euston Station, staring at commuters, like David Attenborough watching a pride of lions on the Serengeti, scrutinising every person he could see and inventing sinister reasons for them being there and carrying the bags and briefcases he was always fantasising about "touching for".

He'd probably think it was time well spent, though, because he got a lot of material for his nightly storytime sessions in The Joy and I've never got half the fucking attention he's getting at the moment.

"So, what happened next?" asks one of the fans.

"Well, she touched for the case and the bloke goes to follow her, but I put the block on him at the door. Just got in his way, to give her enough time to mingle in with the crowds and hop into an auld Jo. Piece of piss, it was."

"So what was in the case?" another one of the other disciples asks.

"Money."

"How much?"

"Twenty grand. I was a bit disappointed, 'cos if it had been gear, we'd have been made for life. We could've retired on it. Gone straight, you know. But sure, twenty grand is twenty grand, I suppose. Every little bit counts."

"Jaysus, that was some scam," said another voice.

"Well, it's instinct, you know. I grew up doing that kind of thing, livin on me wits, being able to spot a switch when it was going down, spot a blag, an opening, an opportunity. You've either got it or you don't."

That's the last straw for me. I decide to deflate the bastard in front of everyone. I can't help meself. "Who was the bird then?" I ask him.

"Sorry?" he says.

"Who was she? The bird who helped you touch for the briefcase."

"Ah, you wouldn't know her," he says, stalling to buy himself a bit of time to think up a name.

"Well, where's she from?"

"Eh, I think she's from Ballymun or somewhere."

"I know loadsa people from The Mun. What's her name?"

"Oh, let me think ... What's her name now? Actually, you probably do know her – Ah, it's on the tip of me tongue ... "

I've destroyed the bastard's credibility and he knows it. As I get up to leave, the rest of the boys are beginning to see him in a different light now.

Then this pang of guilt hits me as I'm walking towards the stairs. I start to wonder to meself why I did that. Johnny was doing no harm to no-one. He's just an auld tin-roofer who robs fifty quid and adds two or three noughts onto the end of it 'cos he wants people to like and admire him. He lies because he's insecure. I mean, how much insecurity could be bred in a person who spends his nights sleeping in shop doorways in London and his days hanging around tube stations waiting for dole day to come around again? What a fucking life.

Don't know why I did it. Well – I do. For the past three weeks, I've been off the gear. Did it the only way you fuckin can. Did it cold turkey. It was bad, but not the worst. Yeh, the paranoia and night-mares were hell and the buckets of sweat, puking and convulsions were no picnic either. But they were a doddle compared to what I'm feelin now – sheer fuckin emptiness. The thing is when you're on the gear you don't feel the monotony of the day in here, of breakfast, dinner and fuckin tea, the same, day in day out. The pool and football and poker, the odd game of span against the wall, a couple of hours of telly and that's your lot. On the gear, you forget that you're goin nowhere. That there's no point to your day. There's no point to *YOU*, for fuck's sake. Only heroin makes you forget that. And only heroin makes you put up with the cunts you meet in here. People like Mad Frankie, who killed another seagull today. They could become an endangered species by the time that sick fucker's let loose on the public again.

As I climb the stairs to bed, I notice that there's a new face on the landing. About twenty-one, I reckon, probably a joyrider and definitely getting his first taste of life in The Joy. You can always tell a newcomer. The look of horror poorly disguised by a thin mask of bravado. This lad's body language is as difficult to read as a Mr Men book. The rest of the lads are swarming around him, lavishing attention on him, like school-kids do when a new boy joins their class in the middle of a term. But their only interest in him is what they can get out of him. "Ye gettin any gear in?" they're asking him. "Tell you what, do a deal, right? You get some in, ye split it with us. When we get it, we'll split it with you, right? That's the way we work things in here, share and share alike, help each other, all pull together."

My arse, it is. But the young fella has such an overwhelming urge to be popular, he tells them just what they want to hear. Yeh, he says, he'll be getting gear in all right. Fuckin plenty of it. Hash, smack, acid, everything. Got contacts on the outside, he has. And share and share alike happens to be his motto, too. "Actually," he says, to a hushed silence, "I might be getting some gear in on Wednesday."

In here, that translates as "I'm definitely getting some gear in on Wednesday" and I make a note in me mind that Wednesday will be the day he gets his first bating. Within an hour of him coming back empty handed from his visit, two or three of his new friends will drag him into a cell and go over him with stainless-steel forks, nail-studded coshes and toothbrushes with blades melted into their handles. My advice is that if you're asked if you're getting gear in, just say no. Tell them you're skint, that you don't have a penny inside or outside, but that if some kind person did happen to bring you in enough for a few turn-ons or a chunk of hash, then you'd give them a shout. You won't win any friends, but you won't make any enemies either.

As I reach the top of the stairs, there's this loud chorus of laughter, real shallow laughter. The boys are all looking at the young fella's charge sheet, as he tells them no doubt some completely unfunny anecdotes about his life in crime. I hate cunts who use their charge sheets as a badge of honour. But there are so many people like Johnny around, no-one believes fuck-all you say until you can somehow get your hands on this piece of paper. Watching this cocky little prick talk his way into a beating has got me thinking now. I don't feel guilty about what I'm after doing to Johnny anymore, because he was no better. If people in here didn't talk so much bollix, then there'd be a lot less trouble.

◆   ◆   ◆

THE RADIO PRIEST

As I lie on me bed in me peter, I know that there's only one thing in the world that can really cheer me up, apart from a turn-on. That Father Michael Cleary fella is on the auld radio tonight with his request show for the prisoners. The letters are always good for a laugh. It's amazing how the smallest things can get you excited when you're inside. I mean, when I was out, the only interest I ever had in radio was robbing the fuckin things out of parked cars to get money for the gear. Now me and the rest of the boys write in to his show regular like, just to hear our names on the air. I turn on the radio and wait for it to start.

There's very few people in here actually like Father Cleary. Everyone just takes the piss out of him in their letters, but he never cops it.

The lads are always writing in under names like "Mike Hunt" and "John Thomas". Cleary must think this fella "Ulick Magee" is real popular too, the number of dedications he gets for him every week.

His first letter tonight is from Barry, a mate of mine. The last line of it reads: "Tell Jacinta I love her very much and not to forget to bring the babby up on the visit." I know what that means, it's Mountjoy-speak for "bring the smack up on the visit" or "bring the smack up on the visit, tucked into a babby's nappy". The priest and the rest of them haven't a fuckin breeze, of course. But we can usually get a good idea of who's getting gear in by tuning in to his show. Barry owes me and I'll be at the top of the queue outside his cell when he gets back from his visit tomorrow to find out what the story is about a turn-on or a bit of blow or whatever he's getting in.

The next letter cracks me up. Browner, another labour day junkie, has written the drippiest load of shite to his bird and Cleary's after reading the whole thing out. It finishes: "Prison gives you a lot of time to think and to get your head straightened out. And I've had the time to realise that I love you very much, Mandy. I'm thinking about you and the babbies every minute of every day. When I get out, thing's are going to be different. I'm going to look after you and make a wonderful life for us to enjoy together." Unless that's code for something, he's gonna get slagged to death in the morning.

"All right, lights and radios off," the screw shouts through me door at eleven o'clock and I flick the light switch, lower the volume on the radio and take the priest into the bed with me, so I can carry on listening. Me indifference towards Father Cleary is turning into a very strong hatred as the show goes on. He's always in The Joy, so he is, visiting and talking to the boys and that. He brought a bunch of lads from town in here a couple of weeks ago to play us in a football match, like, and we kicked lumps off them. Quite a few casualties there were. The thing is, all this "poor misguided souls" crap he talks brings me up in fuckin goosebumps, the like of which I've never known even in me lowest moments of junk withdrawal. There are no misguided souls in this shit-hole of a place. No-one in here has a fucking soul. If I ever had one, I'd have sold it years ago, along with all the tellies and jewellery I robbed to fill me veins with shite.

He's talking to the mother of Kello at the moment. "Ah, your young fella got himself into a bit of trouble, did he?" Cleary's saying. "Ah, how terrible for you. Probably just a phase he went through. But, let he who is without sin cast the first stone ..."

How I wish Kello's love-blind auld one could have been in here last weekend when her misguided son was trying to carve up some poor culchie just because he didn't happen to be born in Dublin. This non-judgemental stuff really gets on my wick. Most of the lads in here would rather be pontificated to than patronised, which is why the priest isn't nearly as popular in here as he likes to think he is. I've built meself into a bit of a rage, so I sit up in the bed and pen a few words to him.

> *Dear Father Michael,*
> *You won't remember me, but I was in the prison last time you visited, although unfortunately we didn't get to talk to each other. Not to worry. I felt I had to write to you to tell you what a great day it was, the football match and that. Sorry the result didn't go your way but, as you know now, there's a few of us in here are a bit handy at the auld ball. Still, it was a really enjoyable day and having you give us that little talk during the tea and biscuits, well, it made me feel a lot happier going back to me cell.*
> *I think I speak for most people in here, Father, when I say that meeting you was a big thrill and I hope we can do it again.*
> *By the way, will you ever get a grip? Your show is fucking brutal, man. Get off the air.*

I sign it "Ulick Magee", slip it into an envelope and address it. I do believe me mood is starting to improve.

♦ ♦ ♦

THE REBEL COUNTY

I've hardly slept a wink tonight. I'm expecting the door to open any minute and the men in the padded gear and helmets to come in and drag me off. Even by my standards, spitting in a screw's face was a stupid thing to do, but he provoked me. Anyway, whatever happens, it was worth the look on the dirt-bird's face when me big greener was dribbling down his cheek and he didn't know whether to leave it there or wipe it off with his sleeve.

The kickers always seem to know instinctively when you've fallen asleep. I'm finally out of it when the door is blown open and before I have a chance to open me eyes, I'm turned over on to me stomach and me arms are twisted up me back. "Don't move," one of them says. Moving is not a fucking option, man. An intensive course in contortionism seems to be part of these cunts' training, because they have managed to tie me up in the kind of knots that struggling would only tighten. The bastards.

They pick me up and run with me like a battering ram along the landing and down the stairs. Where we're going I don't know, because all I can see is the ground flashing past below me, but soon I'm aware that I'm outside. I hear the door of a van being flung open and I'm thrown into the back, face-down on the floor, and ordered not to look up. I'd see fuck-all anyway, sure they've all got helmets with

43

visors on. As the engine starts and we pull out of the main gate, I'm starting to get me bearings. From the voices, I can tell there are five screws in the back with me. One of them sounds familiar, but I just can't put a face to his voice. There's probably a couple more kickers in the front as well. This is a pretty heavy-duty squad they've put together just to move me down to Cork, which is where I presume we're heading.

The kickers say very little on the way down, talking in monosyllables and monotones, anxious as they are to hide their identities. I welcome the peace and quiet and I'm relaxed enough to doze off for what must be a couple of hours. But I have a nightmare. There's four blokes in me cell and they've all got toothbrushes with blades melted into them and they're calling me "Dublin wanker" and "junkie cunt" and I'm backing into a corner and they're getting closer and closer and – I wake up in a sweat. Me nightmare will become reality when I arrive in Cork, nothing fuckin surer.

The first time I was ever in Cork I was in the place about five minutes, strolling up the landing with me blanket, looking for me cell, when a right hook appeared out of nowhere and burst me nose open. Luckily for me I hit the deck, because it was followed by a headbutt, which just about missed me. "More fucking Dubs!" this real aggressive Cork voice shouted. "This place is already bursting. When these cunts are ghosted down here, it means some of our lads are gonna to be moved up to the fucking Joy." Then he booted me in the balls and walked off.

When I got back to Dublin after two weeks of hell, I promised to beat the shite out of every mullah bastard that ever darkened the door of The Joy. And I did. Many's the time me and a few of the other lads ambushed one, dragged him into a cell, threw him to the deck and went about him with our toothbrushes. Just to say, "Welcome to The Joy, don't fuck with the Dubs," you know. But it's at times like this you regret making enemies of those cunts. Knowing my luck, the first person I look at when I walk through that door will be someone I've battered in The Joy. Not that it makes any difference. The only excuse they need to knock the bollix out of you is that you're from Dublin, that's why we return the favour whenever any of the culchies are shanghaied up here.

I manage to get a bit more kip and, when I wake, we've stopped. I hear a voice mention that we've arrived in Cork. I'm looking forward to getting out of this smelly van and into a bed. Then someone says: "We're well on time for the ferry."

I decide it's time for me to talk. "What are we getting the ferry for?"

"Quiet, you," a voice shouts.

I persist, though. "I thought I was going to Cork. You don't need a ferry to go to Cork."

"You're not going to Cork," I'm told.

"Where am I going then?"

"You're going to Spike Island."

I think I'd rather do a year in Cork, with batings and all, than spend a day in Spike. It's supposed to be a prison but it's really just dormitories full of annoying little adolescent pricks who think their joyriding convictions make them hard men. All the bull-shitting I'm going to have to listen to. This is punishment, all right, and I'm not going without a fight. I start to scream at the top of me voice about wanting to see the Cork prison governor. I writhe around on the floor until I'm on me back and then I start kicking out at the screws. But they throw me over on to me stomach again. Then one of the bastards kneels on me back, completely disabling me.

I spend the rest of the journey lying face down on the floor, feeling all sorry for meself as we move on towards the ferry port. Me little show of aggression got me nowhere. But I have another plan. When I get to Spike, I'll just tell them I've got the virus. I'll tell them that if they don't send me back to The Joy, I'm going to start cutting meself and leaving puddles of me dirty blood all over the place. Those bastards won't even bother checking the medical records to see if I'm lying, they'll be that anxious to get me out. The last thing they want on their hands out in Spike is an Aids epidemic. No, I'll have a little chat with the governor down here first thing when he gets into work and I'll be back in Dublin by the time it gets dark again.

♦ ♦ ♦

REFLECTIONS: YOUNG MR FIXIT

I got me first job at sixteen. "Shelf Stacker" was me job description, though me duties involved loads of other interesting things like sweeping, counting plastic bags and opening fuckin boxes. Very bleedin challenging. Me and Jemser went along together. I'd been on the rock 'n' roll since I left school, didn't even want a fuckin job. Just went 'cos Jemser said he'd heard the place was looking for young fellas to stack supermarket shelves at night. Money wasn't bad. Fifty pence an hour. But working from ten at night till six in the morning was a bollix.

"If there's just one job," said Jemser when we were goin in, "I'm on it first, right?"

But there was two going and, after brown-nosing some spotty assistant manager prick for half an hour, we were give a uniform, told what to do, and warned to be back at the supermarket that night, "ten sharp".

That afternoon, I went along to the bloke in town who we used to call the "Mad Barber" to get me head shaved. Racist bastard, he was, but he was cheap. The cunt had pictures of Hitler on the walls and he'd tell you that the Nazis had the right idea and that the Jews that were killed during the War were a waste of good gas. As I sat in the big leather chair that afternoon, his mouth went at the same speed as his electric razor as he ranted on about niggers and Pakis and Spiks and queers and how they should all be shot. I tried me best to ignore him, but he kept catching me eye in the mirror.

"Tell you a joke," he said. "Did you hear about the Jewish child-molester?"

I just shrugged me shoulders, not wanting to encourage the bastard.

"He used to go around in his car, asking kids whether they wanted to buy sweets."

He went into convulsions of laughter and I, like a fucking eejit, smiled at him, out of politeness, like. But the cunt thought he'd found a kindred spirit whom he could bore the ears off for half an hour. I stared at his reflection in the mirror and pictured him at home, dressed up in combat gear, surrounded by pit-bull terriers, wanking himself off to his back issues of *Guns and Ammo*. This urge came over me to tell the fucker what I really thought of him, but he was using an open blade to shave the hairs on the back of me neck, so I thought it best to keep me mouth shut.

Me new haircut and career in the supermarket industry gave me a sense of status among me mates and, as a sort of celebration that night, we all headed into town. *The Exorcist* was on in the pictures. It had been banned everywhere, but somehow some film club or other was allowed to show it. Those arty-farty sorts can get around any-thing, you know. The film was supposed to be a bit gory, but one of the lads suggested getting a few tabs of LSD to make it even scarier. So

47

we sat around in this little derelict shed down the quays, taking acid for the first time and then the eight of us walked into town, as the effects of the drug started to take hold. Mine was a bad trip. Paranoid as fuck, I was. Looking around me throughout the film, thinking every bastard in the pictures was talking about me. Most of the other lads seemed grand. They were just buzzing. I could see snakes and rats and maggots crawling all over the place. I wanted to get out. Then all of a sudden Balfie came back from the jacks, looking really distressed. "The dirt-birds," he was shouting. "The fucking dirt-birds!"

This big chorus of "Ssshhhh" went up. We tried to calm him down.

"I'm after being in the jacks," he said, "and two queers in there felt me hole."

We all knew that the public toilet on O'Connell Bridge used to attract a load of perverts and steamers to the area and they were obviously coming into the pictures now. None of us bothered to ask ourselves whether Balfie had really been felt up or whether the acid had just heightened the cunt's homophobia. We all just burst into the toilet looking to split heads. Inside the door, there were two lads, about nineteen or twenty, sitting down on the floor, chatting away, like. What with their faggoty voices and the earrings in their right ears, there was no need to ask questions. We surrounded them, called them every queer name under the sun and kicked the fuck out them. We all lost control of ourselves, but it was good, like. Being part of a lynch mob, getting caught up in it and that. Me feet were sore from kicking one of the fuckers in the head and then we just left them, a bloodied mess on the floor, the two of them curled up next to each other in the foetal position, like, their blood trickling into the porcelain trough and turning the piss-water red. I went back to work that night still buzzing. I must have packed a fuckin record number of shelves.

Going to the pictures on acid became a regular feature in our lives.

The Adelphi started a Bruce Lee run and a couple of the lads went fucking ballistic after tripping during *Fist of Fury*. Bating down Middle Abbey Street they were, making screeching noises and aiming karate chops and kicks at anyone stupid enough to make eye contact with them. Soon, the acid became more important than the films and then the films became not important at all and we stopped going.

We carried on tripping in the shed, which was where me mate Duffo showed me a bag of heroin for the first time. "A thousand times better than a tab," he said.

I was too frightened of needles to touch it. I remembered, as a kid, the day I ran out of the Health Board screaming me head off when the dentist tried to give me an anaesthetic for a filling. There was no way I could put that needle in me own arm. Duffo said he'd do it for me. He said why not skin pop for the first time, like stick it straight into the skin instead of a vein. I watched him cook the shot up and, when he'd drawn it into the syringe, he told me to roll up me sleeve. He commented on me veins, how well they looked and then he jabbed the needle into the top of me arm, just below the shoulder, and let the stuff go. I suddenly felt all light-headed. Then I felt light all over. Then I felt itchy around me nose, then on me face and then all over me body, until the urge to scratch became too much. Then I puked up the two litres of cider I'd drunk.

The boys all laughed. "Skin-popping doesn't agree with you," Duffo said, doing his best to sound as though he knew what he was talking about. "You'd wanna mainline it next time. Put it straight into your vein. It's a better buzz, man."

The next night, I did. I barfed again, but I still loved it. I was soon shooting up any time I had the money for a ten-pound bag and then I was doing it even when I didn't. Within a few months, we were all so mad into the gear we were going on the rob every night to get the money for a turn-on. Me job in the supermarket began to matter less and less to me and more often than not I wouldn't make it to work at all. They were always down at me door lookin for me. But sure, I was never fuckin in. Cars were easy prey and, to me, every one with a foreign licence plate was a bag of smack just waiting to be collected. American tourists were always stupid enough to believe they could leave wallets and handbags and cameras in their cars in "liddle ol' Areland". We found all sorts of ways to break into them in a few seconds. There were "chop locks", which you could open if you hit them in the right spot with the side of your hand. Then there were "kick locks" which required just a bit of persuasion from the sole of your shoe. We'd roam empty back-streets around town, robbing radios, leather jackets and anything that could be resold or converted into smack.

It was risky, but. Especially when the Old Bill decided to clamp down on inner city crime. One local pig, who we used to call "Sneaky", would crawl under parked cars on the streets we used to target, wait until we arrived to do a job and then stick his hand out and grab a leg. A couple of the boys had been lifted that way. It started to get dangerous.

I didn't give a fuck, because I'd discovered that there were even richer pickings to be had elsewhere. Back at the supermarket, I started robbing stuff from the other lads' lockers. Jemser, who had started using as well, would keep sketch out the back, while I went around with a screwdriver and burst these feeble little brass locks off every cunt's locker. You'd always get a few bob out of them. One night I fecked a nice camera from one locker and grabbed the bloke's leather jacket off his hanger as well, stuffed them inside a bag and pegged it out of the place. I sold them easy enough, but just when I'd started to congratulate meself on committing the perfect crime, the manager and his fuckin pizza-faced assistant were down me gaff the next morning asking questions. "A few items went missing from a locker last night," one of them said.

"What's that got to do with me?" I asked, playing the innocent.

"Were you at the supermarket last night?"

"Sure, you know I was. Wasn't I clocked in?"

"Yeah. But you left with something that you didn't have when you arrived, didn't you?"

I just looked at them blankly. "What are youse talking about?"

"Look, you were seen."

Some cunt must have seen me with a bag that I didn't have coming in that evening. I just kept on denying any knowledge of it, but. Without a confession, the two boys had fuck-all proof and they went away pissed off that they hadn't broken me, but determined now to prove it was me. As me dependency on the gear was growing, me efforts to get the sponds to pay for it were getting more and more reckless.

Then I did something stupid. One night in the middle of the summer, I bursted the manager's locker open and grabbed a load of stuff out of it. Envelopes, wallet, the lot. I stuffed it all up inside me jacket and just walked out of the place. I walked all the way into town and sat on the bank of the canal. I opened one of those envelopes up. There was fuck-all money inside. But then I started shiteing myself. There were all these bunches of fuckin keys in one of the envelopes. Keys to every lock and door in the place. I was gicking meself 'cos, as well as me own bit of robbin, the supermarket had been hit by a couple of armed robberies. They'd fuck-all to do with me, but with the keys on me, I'd be in the frame for them if I was caught. This was heavy fuckin shit. The evidence had to be disposed of. I whipped the money out of the wallet and fucked the keys and the rest of the shite into the canal. Like an idiot, I didn't go back to work for the next week and, since I was already the chief suspect in a number of other robberies, they drew their own conclusions.

I was picked up a couple of weeks later as I was walking along the street. The squad car pulled up alongside me. "I've nothing on me," I said to the cop.

"Get in the car," he said.

"Why?"

"Get in," he said again, this time more firmly and I knew that doing a runner wasn't an option. Another pig hopped out, grabbed me and pushed me into the back of the car. He got on the radio. "We've picked up that bloke for the supermarket," he said.

"What supermarket?" I said. "What the fuck are ye talking about?"

"Things have been going missing," he said, "including some keys. We want to ask you some questions." This cunt thought he was out of "Starsky and Hutch".

We went down the pig station and they led me into this interview room, where they took it in shifts to grill me about the supermarket. They soon copped on, though, that I was just small fry, not up to pulling off an armed raid, not the brains behind some inside job. They'd nothing on me and I was let off.

Unfortunately, the supermarket decided they had to let me go, the fuckers rubbing salt into me wounds by giving auld crater face the pleasure of telling me I was sacked. I decided not to take a case of unfair dismissal against them. Anyway, without a full-time job to get in the way, I could apply now meself whole-heartedly to me career as a junkie.

DETERRENT

THE ALLEY CATS

You can keep your football and your snooker. Handball is the sport for me. Philistines will tell you that it's just a matter of two blokes whacking a small ball backwards and forwards off a wall all day. But no, it's much more than that. Handball, I read somewhere, is a game of skill and finesse and one which requires the most exquisite bodily control and coordination and a range of skills you'll need in few other sports. The screws can't understand its sudden popularity in here. Everyone's mad into it. We're talking junkies, alcos and lads who would usually be too bleedin lazy to boot a Coke can if it was on the ground in front of them. They've all taken to handball like fish to water. They're down here in the alley every day, sweating buckets and lashing the ball off the wall.

Not everyone has reached my level, of course. The Handball Wizard, that's me. But it's through sheer practice. If you're committed, you'll reap the rewards. That's what I say.

Gally is brutal at it. I'm not gonna tell him that you're supposed to cup your hand when you hit the ball, because … well, because magicians never reveal their tricks. And I'm like that Paul Daniels when I've got that little rubber ball in me sights. Gally doesn't even understand the rules, for fuck's sake. Clueless, he is. I'm after explaining to him about twenty times all about foot faults, straddle balls, screen balls, wrist balls and dead ball hinders, but I might as well be talking to the wall in front of us. He pretends he knows what I'm on about and then makes a complete balls of his next serve. He's getting on me wick so much at this stage that I just penalise him and tell him it's my turn to serve now.

He's in a fouler over it, but I just take the ball off him, stand behind the service line, side on to the wall and ask him whether he's ready.

"Ready," he says.

"Play-ball," I say, showing off me knowledge of the jargon. I bounce the ball and hit it at the wall and it comes back fast. Gally's attempt to return it is hopeless and it's bobbled along the ground five or six times before his hand comes within six inches of it.

"What's that?" he asks.

"What do you mean 'what's that'? It's a point to me," I tell him. The eejit doesn't even know where to stand, and I have to march him back to the receiver's line. "Now wait there," I tell him, "and when the ball comes back off the wall, you hit it back in the direction it came from, right?"

He nods. I serve. Gally moves more quickly this time, but no more graciously and, as he stoops low to hit it, he falls flat on his face. I can tell there's not going to be many long rallies in this game. When he dusts himself down, I serve again. It's an ace. Then comes another. Then another.

"Will ye give me a fuckin chance?" he says, gasping for his breath. He's sweating like a fuckin mugger in line-up now.

I don't give chances, though. Handball is like life. It has its winners and it has its losers. I am king down here and this is my court. I am ruthless. I am a single-minded, high-powered, iron-fisted winning machine. I can crush this loser any time I want to. I think I want to now, because I'm bored toying with him. It's no contest, you know. He sounds like he's about to have an asthma attack and looks as though he's about to fall over. So I take the ball in me hand one last time and get ready to end the game. I check me watch. It's bang on three. I bounce the ball hard and, as it comes up again, I scoop it high into the air. It just about clears the wall.

"Butter-fingers," Gally grins at me. I smile back at him, we both look around to see whether any screws are about and then both race towards the wall. "Hey, throw us the ball back, will ye?" we call out a few times.

It's not long before a ball comes hurtling over, though it's not the same ball this time. For a start, it doesn't bounce. It hits the ground like a ball-bearing falling on a mahogany floor. We have a quick sketch around again. None of the screws have noticed. I pick it up and pull at the split in it. Inside, there's a package. I remove the clingfilm from it and check whether the smack's all there. It's there all right. About two-hundred worth by the looks of it, just as Dicey said there'd be. I'll stick it up me hole now in a sec and then get one of the cleaners to drop it over to Dicey's cell later on. After I've taken out me share, of course.

Oh yeh, I love handball. As I said, it's a game of incredible finesse and one which requires the most exquisite bodily control and coordination and a range of skills you'll see in few other sports. But practice makes perfect. By the time I get out of here, I'll be able to give the great Ducksie Walsh a good run for his money.

♦　♦　♦

DUBLIN ON £1.66 A DAY

I'm bursting with excitement. When they open that gate, I'm out of here like a bleedin wild horse out of a paddock. Just a few formalities to get through now and then outside world here I come. I've been a good boy lately and this is my reward. The screw behind the counter's filling in this form which is headed "Criminal Justice Act, 1960". When he's finished, he turns it around to me and tells me to sign it.

"Just before you do," he says, "this is your first time on temporary release, isn't it?"

I tell him it is. And I've gotta admit I'm very grateful to the prison authorities for letting me out on TR. They do that when you get near the end of your stretch inside to help you get used to life outside. I'll use me time wisely, of course – see me mates, pick up some quality gear, do a few jobs, like.

"Well, in that case, I'll just draw your attention to the conditions you're required to comply with during the period of your release."

I don't know what the fuck he's talking about, but he points out to list of dos and don'ts on the form and tells me to read them. I snigger to meself as I do:

1. That you shall keep the peace and be of good behaviour during the period of your release.
2. That you shall be of sober habits.
3. That you will not convey any message, written or verbal, into or out of Mountjoy Prison.
4. That you shall report to the Welfare Officer as directed by him/her.
5. That you report back to Mountjoy Prison on (given date and time).
6. That you reside at home.
7. That you report to your local Garda Station daily.

I make meself a little pledge to break as many as I can during the three days they're letting me out for. When I've put me name to it, the screw tears a yellow carbon copy off the back of it and hands it to me. "Now, money," he says. I smile and rub me hands.

"You have £50 you've saved up in gratuity money and £29 in private cash as well."

"Great," I tell him, "I'll take it all."

"No, you won't," he says without looking up at me. "You're only allowed five pounds."

"A fucking fiver? What's the story here, man?"

"You're only being let out on temporary release. You can't touch the rest of your gratuity money or your private cash until you're given full release."

"But that's my bleedin money. I earned it."

"I'm sorry, they're the rules."

Me bollix, are they the rules. It's supposed to be up to the discretion of the prison. If it was some respectable bloke who only got in here because he was fuckin led astray, then he'd be given more than a fiver. It's only 'cos I'm a fucking junkie that they won't give me any more. Still, fuck him. I'll get money from somewhere.

I take me form and me fiver and I'm marched down to the first gate with Duffo, Quinner and Padser, who all seem as excited as me about getting out for the few days. We're chattering away among ourselves, like, while the guy gets on the blower to the man on the front gate and tells him that four lads are to be let out.

As we walk out the gate, we all instinctively know where we're going. There are some things you don't have to be told. Birds migrate in the winter to some place where they're not gonna be freezing their balls off and, for lads out on TR, heading to the off-licence comes just as natural. We buy a two-litre each. It's £4.20 for a bottle of cider now. Some things certainly have changed while I've been in. Ten minutes out of The Joy and I've only got eighty pence left to get me through the next three days. I don't give a shite, though, 'cos money's no problem to come by.

We head off to the park down the road with our gargle and climb over the railings. It's freezing. Real brass monkey weather. We find a bench, sit down and start slagging each other and having the laugh. The cider tastes beautiful compared to the hooch we've been drinking for the last few years and I'm starting to feel merry after a few mouthfuls. Duffo says he's heading into town after to see Tootser about getting a lay-on, a bit of smack on a take now/pay later basis. He asks me whether I'll head in with him, but I tell him I've other plans. That's a lie. It's nothing to do with not liking Duffo or anything. We've known each other since we were young fellas. In fact, he gave me me first turn-on. It's just – I just don't like some of the company he keeps these days. Tootser's a cunt basically. He'd make you chew your own prick off for a bit of smack if he thought you were desperate enough. He hates me anyway for some reason, so I'd have no chance of getting gear off him without any moolah.

As we're talking and drinking, a cop car pulls up outside the park. "Some nosey bitch is after reporting us," I say. Two big pigs get out and call us over to the railings.

"What are you doing?" one of them asks. He's a thick culchie fella.

"We're sitting here having a few drinks to celebrate," I say, showing him me release form. "We're just after getting out of The Joy for a few days."

"Well," the other fella says, "you'll be back in The Joy unless you stay out of trouble and stop bothering people. No messing about. Get yourselves off home." Then he sneers at us. "I'm sure your families will be delighted to see you."

The two of them get in the car, sniggering to themselves, and we call them a few names under our breath. We finish off the dregs in our bottles and decide to head off. Quinner volunteers to go with Duffo to find Tootser and I'm lumbered with Padser, worse luck. He's a sound enough fella. A stroker, mostly handbags and that, to feed his habit. But when I'm out trying to score, the last thing I want is a partner in crime, because if you get a turn-on and they don't, then you're made to feel like the most miserly cunt in the world. Which I probably am anyway, but I don't care. Padser is excess baggage to me. We walk around for a bit, stop off at the pig station to sign on and then head off to try to score.

Someone had told me inside that me auld mate Fitzer had started dealing, which came as a bit of a shock. I didn't even know the cunt was using. I couldn't believe it. Fitzer is selling gear. A fella who was so into fitness and his country and getting himself a career in the pigs until they blew him out because he wasn't tall enough. Un-fuckin-believable. Still, I'm not too blind to see how his misfortune could be my advantage. Me and Padser meet his brother on the stairs on the way up to Fitzer's flat and he tells us he's dealing over the other side of town this afternoon. When we eventually catch up with him, it's like I've never known the guy before. He's changed and I'm not just talking about his wasted appearance. He treats me like a fucking stranger, like just another junkie looking to score.

"If it's a turn-on you're after, it's twenty quid," he says, looking straight through me.

"Any chance of a lay-on?" I say with over-the-top politeness.

"Fuck-all," he says, real cold, like.

I just can't believe this is the bloke I remember. I'm probably after changing as much as he has. Or maybe neither of us has changed. Maybe it's just our relationship that's changed. He's in a position of power, of control. Nothing personal. Just business. How many times have I heard that? The fucker. I start exchanging a bit of small-talk with him about the old days to try to establish some common ground between us and when I begin to see a faint flicker of the old Fitzer in his eyes, I ask him again about an auld lay-on. "I'm just after getting out of The Joy," I tell him, "and I'll pay you back tomorrow when I get me labour. Tell you what, I've a leather jacket up in me gaff, right? I'll drop it down to you, right? I'm getting me labour tomorrow and I'll give you the score back out of that. If I don't, you can hang on to the leather."

He just stares through me. "Please, I'm desperate," I say, committing the cardinal sin of any junkie trying to score.

The fucker feels I've grovelled enough. "Listen," he says, "you don't have to gimme your jacket. I'll give you a turn-on now and you can pay me tomorrow ... But I'm not giving your mate a lay-on, right?"

I look back at Padser, who's keeping a discreet distance. "Fuck him," I say. "It's every man for himself. He'll have to fix himself up."

Fitzer gives me the package. "Gimme the money tomorrow, right?"

"I will, I swear."

As I go to walk away, he asks me: "Have ye got a clean spike?"

"A clean one?"

"Yeh, here ye are," he says, handing me a little package. "Ye can't be too careful these days, what with Aids and that."

Jaysus, I have been away a long time – a lot changes in four years. "Does no-one share any more?" I ask.

"No need," he says. "Sure, there's an exchange programme down Merchant's Quay."

He shouts after me as I walk off. "You better have that score for me tomorrow or you're a fuckin dead man."

Padser catches up with me. "What's the story? Did ye get a couple of lay-ons?"

"He'd only gimme one," I tell him. "I'm after being begging him to give you one as well, but the cunt wouldn't listen. I'm sorry, man. I did me best for ye."

He nods as though he appreciates me efforts. He doesn't need to be told to fuck off, fair play to him. He knows that I've got to go off now and do what I have to do. Watching someone else shoot up when you've no turn-on yourself is no fun.

I go up to me gaff and me ma and da aren't in, which gives me a bit of time to root around for me old works and get this shite into me. I find it in the pocket of me wax jacket hanging up in me old wardrobe. The last time I had it out, there were four or five of us using it and, remembering Fitzer's advice, I give it a good rinse out in the bathroom sink. I go out to the kitchen for a spoon. I open the drawer and notice that none of the spoons matches any other piece of cutlery me ma has. That's because I've had to replace so many of them over the years there's fuck-all of her original set left. A fair few of these ones came from the fast-food place down the road. The bollix of a manager barred me eventually 'cos I was always going in, ordering a cup of tea and then walking out an hour later with me pockets stuffed with sachets of vinegar and spoons.

I decide to use one of them to cook up this shot, just for old times sake, like. I take it into the jacks and lock the door behind me. There's a small plastic Armitage Shanks crest on the cistern which I pull out, leaving a little circular hole in the porcelain. I get down on me knees, bend the handle of the spoon in half and slip it into the hole with the roundy bit jutting out, which frees up both me hands to cook the gear. I heat it with me lighter and stir it with the tip of the needle, which is something I don't usually make a habit of, but I'm dying to get this stuff into me to find out whether the stuff out here's any better than the shite we're getting in The Joy.

The particles aren't as stubborn as I expected and I don't even need to use vinegar to get them to dissolve. I draw the solution up into the works, take the new spike out of its packet and attach it and then sit on the seat of the jacks. I spike a vein in me right arm, draw some red and then ram the stuff into me. I sit back, me head resting against the wall. It's good. It's ... It's not great. Me expectations might have been too high. The smack out here is obviously being cut as much as the gear we're getting inside. I start to feel a bit queasy and I fall onto me knees again and whip the toilet seat up just in the nick of time. I start throwing me ring up. All that cider I drunk earlier comes gorging out. When I've puked up two litres of vomit and me stomach's empty, I retch a couple of times, which hurts and then I fall down onto me hands and knees, propping me cheek against the porcelain to try to cool me face down. After about half an hour or so, I get it together and manage to get up again.

The next morning, I go down the labour and this really severe looking hatch clerk tells me I'm not entitled to a bleedin penny because I'm only out for three days. She suggests I go up to the Eastern Health Board to beg those cunts for a few bob. I don't want to, but I decide to brave it. When I finally get to talk to the community welfare officer, she's just as I remembered her before, an ugly, humourless battle-axe, who goes on as if it's her own bleedin money she's dishin out. I treat the bitch in the trouser suit with all due reverence, though, and for me trouble she gives me twenty-two quid to do me the three days. After the trial of having to be pleasant to her for twenty minutes, I'm gutting for a smoke and I go into the first newsagents I can find to get forty blue and a few auld sweets. It's only when I get me change back that I realise I've broken into the score I owe Fitzer. I've only got seventeen-odd pound left. I go back up the estate, track him down and tell him that that seventeen quid was all the boot the Health Board would give me and he seems to appreciate me honesty.

But I'm skint again. I know I'm going to have to do a job. Since I'm in the estate, I decide to go and knock up Rods. He's a bit thick, but he's a deadly little driver and he's always on for a robbery. Petrol stations and newsagents are his speciality. He's not in when I call to his door, but his sister tells me he's after going out with a screwdriver on him, so I know that he's going to come back with a hot car. I sit on a wall and wait, smoking a good hole in me forty blue. At around midday, he arrives in an auld Ford.

"Are ye doing a job?" I ask him. He just nods his head.

"Are ye on yer Sweeney, are ye?"

"Well, I've no-one with me yet. You can come along if you want."

"What are ye doin?"

"A jumpover. A newsagent's shop."

I climb into the front passenger seat and he tells me he wants to hit the shop at around two in the afternoon. There's a big midweek carry-over on the lottery tonight, so there'll be quite a bit of cash in the gaff. "I'll drive the car and keep sketch at the door of the shop and you get the money," he says, handing me a claw hammer. "Whoever's behind the counter, right, if they give you any shit at all, just hit them over the head with that. No messing around, right?"

He pulls out a lump hammer then, which he explains we'll use to smash the side windscreen of any good citizen who tries to ram us on the road when we're making our getaway. I'm impressed by the amount of planning that's gone into this job.

I think two o'clock will never come and me heart's pounding like a pneumatic drill by the time we reach the shop. Rods pulls up outside, but turns off the engine. "Bollix," he says, "there's too many people hanging around the bookies' across the road. Must be a big race on. They'll suss us straight away if they see us leaving the car ticking over there with a screwdriver in the ignition."

"Why don't we come back later?" I ask him. "What about half-seven? There'd be a fortune in the Lotto till by that time."

"Fuck that, the shop'd be packed at that time. It's a big jackpot to-night. No, we'll come back at four o'clock, so we just avoid the rush-hour traffic."

We drive back to the estate and talk about the job again, which just makes me more nervous. I'm farting me arse off and I have to wind down the window. Half-three finally comes and we drive off in the direction of the newsagent's. This time, there's hardly any cars parked outside.

"Right, let's do it," Rods says. I pull on a woolly that he has in the car and wrap a scarf around me face to cover me nose and mouth. When the last customer leaves the shop, I grip the hammer hard and Rods shouts, "Let's fuckin do it!"

We make a rush for the door. The young one behind the counter screams as soon as she sees me running towards her. The adrenalin just takes me over. I leapfrog the counter, grab her and start pulling her around by the hair. She's screaming and crying and shouting, "No, no, no, please no," over and over again. Bitch probably thinks I'm gonna rape her. I just hold the hammer up to her face. "All I'm wanting is the money!" I scream. "Gimme it, or I'll smash your fuckin head in!"

She tries to open the Lotto till, but the little wagon's hands are shaking too much. The thing is, I'm just as frightened as she is. "I'll fucking do you!" I shout again.

"Get the fucking money and come on!" Rods is shouting. He's turned around, facing the door. Another bloke comes charging down the stairs at the back of the shop. "It's okay," he says, "I'll open the till. Just don't hurt her."

Lucky for her he came. He opens it up and I grab a fistful of notes and stuff them into me pocket, leaving the change behind. "What about the other till!" I shout to Rods.

"No time," he says. "Come on, just leave it."

I jump back over the counter. We hop into the car and speed off, with Rods doing justice to his reputation as a good wheels man. I count out the money on me lap. There's £280 altogether. That's £140 each. Rods seems happy with the 50/50 split.

We get back to the flat, divvy it up and go our separate ways. I score some more gear down Cook Street and shoot up in me gaff again. In the evening, I go up to me local to buy a round of drinks to celebrate me few days of freedom. I've another twenty pound turn-on in me pocket for the morning and enough for gargle tomorrow night as well. All in all, I think you could say, I've done well out of me fiver.

♦   ♦   ♦

MARTINA? DON'T ASK

Martina. She was me first love. We had known each other for donkey's years. I'd always been keen on her. She was a good-looking bird, but she always gave the impression that she didn't try or didn't have to try. Maybe that's what attracted me most to her. It was her free spirit, her independence. Somehow, she didn't seem to need anyone and that quality seemed to draw people to her. Me most of all. It didn't take people long to suss out that I was mad into her. The way I'd drop her name, real casual, like, the way I'd probe people for information about her, the way I'd take a redner whenever she was around.

It was the gargle that gave me the courage to hold me first conversation with her in a pub near the estate. I can't remember what I said to her, but it worked because she laughed and then she blushed and we had eyes and words for only one another until last orders were called.

As I walked her up to her landing that night and kissed her for the first time, I knew I'd discovered something I cared about at least as much as smack. We were inseparable after that. Except for the times I'd be out with the lads, breaking into cars or robbing the toy factory down on the quays with the two guard dogs that used to leg it when you made a run at them. Apart from that, me and Martina did everything together. We both agreed it was love.

But things wouldn't always be like this, we knew. Me case was about to come up. I had been lagged for another jumpover I did. The trial would be a formality. I was going down, but didn't know how long for. When the judge said five years, I don't know how I stayed standing in the dock. As they led me down, I turned back and took a last look at Martina, who was roaring her eyes out and shaking her head in disbelief. She came to see me in The Joy a couple of days later and she was roarin crying, all upset, so I told her she wasn't to wait for me. I was the one serving the sentence not her and she had to go on living. I didn't mean a fuckin word of it but, for once in me life, I was putting someone else's interests ahead of mine.

Didn't matter, because she wouldn't hear of it. She kept going on about how I was the only bloke she'd ever genuinely loved and how she'd wait for me even if I had to serve life. Every week, she came to see me without fail and we used to sit in the visiting room holding hands, pitying anyone who wasn't as much in love as we were.

You'd always see the odd bloke in the visiting room crying like a baby as his bird tells him that she has been unfaithful or that she has fallen in love with someone else. That there was nothing she could do. That it just happened. Then he'd put his head on her shoulder and cry and cry and cry. Then he'd plead with her. And if that didn't work, he'd threaten to do himself in when he got back to his cell. The lowest form of bribery, but you had to understand how helpless these guys felt, already knowing that they couldn't satisfy the women they loved, and then torturing themselves wondering whether anyone else was.

You could sit in your cell at night, wondering whether she was out on the town with her mates, maybe meeting up with a gang of lads and going on to a nightclub. Wondering whether someone was trying to chat her up. A handsome, well-mannered, rich and charming guy, maybe. You wonder what witty lines he's using on her and how she's responding. Then you scratch it all out of your head. But soon you find yourself thinking about the milkman and that time you caught him staring at her. And the television repair man who has had to call to the house twice this week. And your mates down the local who ...

None of it matters a fuck though if you're in love, if you're really in love. While I missed Martina like mad, I never asked her about what she did at night or during the day. All we talked about was the future.

I knew she was excited about something that Tuesday afternoon a couple of months into me sentence when she came to visit. She always smiled when she saw me, but this was somehow broader, brighter. Before I'd even had a chance to sit down, she told me. She was pregnant. Three months gone. We were going to have a baby. We hugged and kissed each other for about ten minutes and we both started to cry. I was speechless, but I wouldn't have got a word in edgeways anyway, 'cos she just went into overdrive, talking about everything we were going to do for our child. She was going to paint the other bedroom in the flat and turn it into a nursery. I was going to get off the gear, when I got out. I was going to get a job and settle down and be a responsible parent. She went down to me da's local that night to break the news to him and they had a few pints together, just to wet the baby's head like.

But then something happened. It was a couple of days later, during rec. One of the lads said he was sorry to hear about me and Martina splitting up. "What are ye talking about?" I asked.

"I hear she's with Rat Boy now."

"Me mate, Rat Boy?"

"Yeh."

"Not at all," I said. "We're still together. Sure, we're having a baby, for fuck's sake."

"Oh, sorry, I must have got it arseways."

"You must have. Me and Martina are grand."

Suddenly, me mind started to work in the same way as all those other blokes I'd seen crying in the visiting room. I thought about Martina. No, she seemed too happy to be playing around. But what happened when she was out with me da that night? Did she go on anywhere after? A nightclub maybe. With Rat Boy. Rat Boy, me mate. Rat Boy, the cunt. He was always a ladies' man, not an ugly fucker by any stretch of the imagination and always able to turn on the auld charm, the auld one-liners coming easy to him. Rat Boy ... Nah, he wouldn't. Sure, I'd asked him to look after her. And she wouldn't either. Not with the babby on the way. Not when she's so happy either. And she was so happy when she was in.

Me da broke the news to me. He was standing up when I got into the visiting room, looking sad. For a minute, I thought he was going to tell me that me ma was ill or something.

"Sit down, son," he said, putting his hand on me shoulder.

"What's wrong, Da? Is it me ma?"

"No, it's nothing like that. I've got something to tell you. I want to tell you before someone else does."

"Yeh?"

"It's Martina."

"Martina? Oh fuck, is she all right? Is it the baby?"

"No, listen to me, son. She's – She's with ..."

"Rat Boy," I said.

He nodded. "He's moved into the flat with her. I'm so sorry, son."

I can't remember anything else we said to each other. Da hugged me but knew there was nothing he could say to console me. I picked up the smokes and the papers he'd dropped me in and walked back to me cell. I lay down on me bed and cried for hours.

It's only now that Martina's plucked up the courage to come in and tell me to me face, but I'm not sure if I'm ready to see her. I have to. The screw unlocks me door and tells me I've a visitor. For about thirty seconds, I refuse to move.

"Do you want to see her?" he asks in a kindly voice.

"Yeh, all right," I tell him.

As soon as I see her, all the things I've been planning to say are gone out of me mind. She doesn't stand up. There's no hug. No kiss. "How are ye?" she asks, as if she gives a fuck.

I don't answer. "Why did you do it to me, Martina?" I ask her.

"Look, neither of us wanted it to happen. It just did. I was lonely. I needed someone. Rat Boy was just there."

"So when did it start? How did it start?"

"Telling you won't do any good."

"It'll fuckin make me feel better. So come on. What is it he has?"

"We ... We love each other."

"Last week, you loved me."

"It wasn't love ... I mean– What I mean is, it wasn't love like this."

"So what's the fucking difference?"

"Look, you were the one who said you didn't expect me to wait for you."

"But you said you would."

"I know, but I didn't know it would be so difficult. You're the one serving the fuckin sentence. You were the one stupid enough to get fucking caught. You can't expect me to stop living. Am I supposed to stay in every night of the bleedin week? I'm young, I want to go out and have fun, have a laugh, a few drinks, meet people."

"Meet other blokes."

"I didn't want to hurt you."

"Why did you then? Why did you come in here and tell me all that bollix about the babby and the flat and how we were going to start a new life together once I got out. Winding me up in prison. And why did you drag me fuckin family into it? Why did you go out with me da and tell him and then tell me ma as well, knowing how happy they'd be and knowing that you were just gonna pull the fucking rug from under them?"

She had that scolded child look on her face. "I don't know," she shrugged.

I thought that tears might help. "Look, Martina, can't we just forget about this and go back to the way we were?"

"No," she says, hard as nails.

"Why not?" I sob. "Martina, I love you. And I don't think I'll be able to make it through these next few years in here if I know there's nothing at the end of it. Please, Martina. I'm begging you."

A tear runs down her cheek. She clasps my hand. "It's over," she says, before getting up to leave.

"Fuck you," I mutter under me breath. She doesn't seem to hear. I watch the screws let her out and she doesn't look back at me. I sit there moping for about ten minutes and notice that there's another guy sobbing beside me. His bird, who's as calm as anything, sits there across from him. He catches me eye and gives me this knowing look, as if to say he knows what I'm going through. As I stand up and go back to me cell, all me thoughts about Martina start to go sour. I think about the baby. With all the upset, I forgot to ask her whether it was mine. Stupid question anyway. What the fuck does it matter?

◆　◆　◆

BLOOD BROTHERS

It was wrong. We all said it. 'Course it was. A bloke should be able to see his bird if she's just after having a babby. Gibbo claims he has the virus. Could be the last chance he ever gets to see them. Bloke should be able to see his bird and his babby. End of story.

But Gibbo is no ordinary bloke. He's a bleedin headcase, with a love of knives and a lust for using them to cut people up, including himself. Sure, he's only after starting a seven-stretch for half-killing some bus driver. He jumped into the bus, sat up near the front and chatted away to the driver as they went along and then whipped out a Stanley knife. He held it to the bloke's throat and told him he'd cut him from ear to ear unless he gave him the night's takings. So the driver, gicking himself like, handed over all his notes, no questions asked. But before he went, Gibbo slashed his throat anyway, the crazy bastard.

There's no trusting someone like that. I mean, he's mentally defective. No arguments. There's always tension in here when he's around. If you're halfway through a frame of snooker and he decides he wants to play, you just forget your own match, hand him your cue, rack up the reds and spot the colours for him and get the fuck out of his sight before he accuses you of staring at him and batters you. You can't relax when he's there, you know. The screws are too scared to bring him out to the hospital, babby or no babby. They reckon it would take an operation involving military-style planning, a convoy of cars, helicopters and thirty screws all on danger-money to bring him out and even then they'd have to seal off all the streets around to foil his inevitable escape plan.

The Governor told him that considering the security risk it would pose, they couldn't agree to it. Gibbo just went spare. Supposed to have started spitting blood all around the place. That's pretty serious shit, especially 'cos he's supposed to have the virus and that. Someone said he slipped a bit of a blade into the side of his mouth and cut the inside of his cheek with it when he didn't get his own way. So the screws squeezed him into a strait-jacket and left him cursing and writhing around in the padded cell till he calmed down.

They should have sent him straight back up to Dundrum, where he's spent most of his prison career anyway. The screws should have known that once he had decided to get out of The Joy he'd do it. And he'd do it the way he always did, by doing damage to himself. Gibbo's one of those blokes who has never come to terms with the fact that he's going to be locked up for a long time and he lies awake at night, hatching these fuckin stupid escape plans, most of which revolve around the hospital, where he imagines security is more lax. The pain the mad bastard will inflict on himself just to get out there is incredible. When he's stripped to his jocks, his body is just one ugly mass of scar tissue. There's hardly an inch of flesh that hasn't been cut open at some stage or other, either by himself during his many self-infliction frenzies, or by surgeons operating to remove some of the objects he's swallowed in his time.

They've pulled those AA-size batteries out of him, two or three at a time, as well as nails and razor blades. He's drunk so much disinfectant, Jeyes fluid and bleach in the last couple of years, he doesn't even get sick when he does it any more. Immune to toxins, he is. He once swallowed the steel springs off his bed. The joke in here is that the screws don't have to spend any money on security when he's in the hospital. They just have to put one of those metal detector yokes that you have to walk through at the airport on the front gate. Gibbo's escape plans have never come to anything, because by the time he gets to the hospital, he's usually too sick to try anything. And anyway, the screws have been wise to him for years. That's why I'm surprised they didn't send the mad bastard off to The Drum when he went apeshit.

73

We all knew something bad was going down from the moment they let him out of the pad. You could feel the tension. It took about five minutes for it to happen. It started with this piercing scream. Gibbo and his mate, Anto, who is just as crazy, were running amok with the razor blades. One screw was already lying on the ground bleeding and the two boys were running towards the spiral staircase. Another screw, who had the misfortune of being on it at the time, was stabbed in the leg and arm, before he managed to dive head first over the banister just as they were about to do his face.

The two lads clambered up on to the big wire cage that overhangs the prison like a couple of chimpanzees and they sat down on the tiny ledge at the top of it, swinging their legs. No-one knew what would happen next. A whole army of screws arrived and it was obvious that a bit of a siege was developing. Gibbo started shouting down to them. "All I wanted to do was see me bird and me kid, right? And yiz wouldn't let me, yiz bastards. Yiz are gonna be sorry, do ye hear me?"

Then he started calling out the screws by name. "I'm gonna make sure I give yiz all Aids before I get out of this place, right?"

Gibbo had rolled up his sleeves and was holding the blade to the inside of his wrist. Then he shouted: "Yiz're gonna pay for this. Don't make any plans for Christmas, 'cos you're not gonna see it. Welcome to the club, lads."

A single drop of blood hit the floor, followed by another and then another, splashing like rain on the tiled floor. Then it started to pour down. Anto started slicing his arms up too.

"Yiz are wasting your time hanging around, 'cos I'm not climbing down from here!" Gibbo shouted. "I'll fall down eventually, though."

The screws were suddenly very anxious to get us all back into our cells. Maybe they thought that Gibbo might start a full-scale riot, so they came up to the landings and started to shepherd us into our peters. Gibbo's voice was full of hate. "Where are youse going, yiz shiters?" he said. "They wouldn't even let me out to see me bird and me kid. I'm gonna die and I'm never gonna see them again. They're bastards. They'll be doing it to youse next week. Don't go back for them. Don't do an'thin they tell yiz to."

We were all kind of emotionally blackmailed into staying, like. But we just stood around on the landing, unsure of what we were supposed to be doing, just watching.

"Come on, lads, tear the place up!" Anto was shouting.

There was this horrible silence. The place was on the brink of all-out war. All it would have taken was one person to hit one of the screws a box and it would have gone up. Most of us secretly wanted to riot, not because we were outraged at the way that psychotic bastard up there had been treated, but just to break the sheer monotony of life in here. No-one had the balls to throw the first dig, and the moment passed.

"Fuckin wreck the joint!" Gibbo was shouting. "Yissel all get out, so yiz will. Batter those bastards and break out."

It wasn't a bad idea. It was just the fact that it was being suggested by a couple of looneys who were carving up their arms like joints of rump beef that persuaded us not to. Anto taunted us: "Chickens!"

Gibbo's jeans had changed from light blue to a deep crimson colour. The small pools of blood smattered around the floor were starting to run into each other and form large puddles, as the two lads laughed like maniacs. It wasn't a spectator sport. One by one, we quietly slinked off back to our cells.

As I lie on me bed, I can still hear Gibbo shouting. "I want to talk to the Minister for Justice. I'm not coming down until I see the Minister for Justice down there in the circle!" I don't manage to sleep with all the shouting and insane cackling that carries on right the way through the night. Never mind. When they come down, they'll stitch them up and pack them off to the fuckin Drum again, hopefully for good this time. The Bomb Squad will be around in the morning to mop up the puddles and soon there'll be nothing left to remind us that they were ever here.

◆ ◆ ◆

A BAD TRIP

Tooler comes to me door. "What's the story with the works, man?"

I just lose me rag with the cunt. "You'll have it when I say you can have it." He goes off in a snot. The thing is, I'm stalling on purpose. The fucker's so strung out he'd get down and lick me balls to get me works off me and we both know it. Nothing personal against the guy, right? This is just one of the petty power games junkies play. I get few enough opportunities to feel important, so it has to be enjoyed while it lasts.

Me ma dropped me in a copy of The Eagles' greatest hits today and I'm doing exactly what Glen Frey suggests. I'm taking it easy. While I'm doing this, I'm also cooking up a shot. The auld morphine sulphate tablets, or napps as we call them, wouldn't have been me first choice. (Give me uncut Colombian brown any day of the week.) The napps are used to treat cancer patients and are every bit as strong as smack, but. Or so I'm told, although it's true that I've only ever heard dealers say it, so it's probably bollix. But beggars can't be choosers and anyway, for me twenty-five quid, I've managed to get a few one-hundred strength ones, the strongest on the market.

I'm listening to that "Hotel California", a song that I read somewhere is about the decadence of Californian life. I think it was in the *NME*. I smile quietly to meself at the irony of cooking up gear in The Joy while I'm listening to songs about mirrors on ceilings and pink champagne on ice. I sing along to Henley on vocals. All about checking out, but never being able to leave. Fuck me, those lines could have been written about this place.

Tooler's back again, just mooching around outside, too scared to come in in case he pisses me off and too frightened to go back to his cell and wait in case I give the works to someone else. I decide to end the little game, not to put the pathetic little fucker out of misery, but because he's gonna start drawing the screws' attention to me cell. The shot is still hot on the spoon, but I suck it up into the barrel through me filter, attach me spike and puncture a vein in me left arm. I try to suck some blood back into the barrel, but the thing is jammed for some reason and it won't go back. I may have hit a blood clot, but I just push forward instead, releasing the mixture slowly but deliberately. I sit back on me piss-pot and savour the hit. It feels fucking good, man. I feel so ... It's great gear, all right. True what they say about it. So good, it is, I'm too out of it to pull me bleedin works out of me arm.

After what must have been a couple of minutes, Tooler comes in and pulls it out for me. He goes off with it, calling me a bollix under his breath, which is a fuckin testament to the shift in the balance of power between us now. I don't answer him back, because suddenly I'm feeling a bit Moby Dick. I don't know what it is. Something's not right with me, that's all I know. It starts in me auld Ned Kelly, a pain, like. I move over to the bed and lie down, expecting it to pass, but it doesn't. Me feet start tingling with the pins and needles. The sensation spreads up me legs quickly and through the rest of me body. Then it starts getting more and more severe, until it feels like me whole body is covered in one great big rash of blisters, and they're burning into me flesh like a fuckin branding iron. But I'm trembling with the cold as well. I sit up on the bed and struggle to me feet. After managing three or four steps forward, I have to look down to make sure they're touching the ground, because I can't feel them. Me legs either. I'm paralysed from the waist down now and it's as though I'm standing on thin air. I feel like that coyote out of the Road Runner cartoon, the one who runs off cliff edges and manages to run along in mid-air for five or six seconds before he finally falls to the ground. I'm standing here like a bleedin statue for what seems like ages, until Redser comes in and asks me what's wrong.

"I'm fuckin scared, man, I can't feel me legs." There's panic in me voice. "I can't feel me legs. I can't feel me legs. I'm in bits."

"Must be a dirty hit," Redser says. "Lie down quick."

He helps me stagger backwards, lays me out on the bed and rolls me over onto me side, just in case I puke in me sleep. "What do ye think happened?" he asks me.

"Dunno. The stuff was still hot when I put it in me. And I think I hit a blood clot as well ... I'm fuckin scared, man."

"You'll be all right," he says, "just let it run its course and you'll be sound."

I don't think I ever could be again. Me pores are pumping out icy water instead of sweat and me shirt, which is dripping now, clings to me skin underneath me jumper. The sensation is fucking horrible. It's like withdrawal, only worse. The shivering has got more pronounced now and me body is going into these spasms. "Throw us your duvet over, will ye?" I ask him.

"Don't be bleedin stupid," he says. "If the screws come in and find you like this, they'll know you've had a bad trip. You'll be in shit then."

"I'm in shit now, Redser. Go on, give us yours over. I'm freezin me balls off here."

He throws his duvet over me own. "What are you gonna do about rec?" he asks. "You can't go down for it in that state."

"Do us a favour, will ye? Just tell the screws I've got a headache and I'm tryin to sleep it off."

In that state of mind somewhere between consciousness and unconsciousness, I start to think about Billy. Horrible fuckin thoughts that no amount of tossing and turning can stop. It wasn't my fault. I did everything I could. It was years ago. Me and Billy had scored some Diconal, these small pink tablets that looked a bit like the auld Junior Disprins. You never knew what you were gonna get off them. It all depended on what you mixed them with. I'd taken four once and got fuck-all buzz, but I knew lads who had nearly OD-ed on one of them. There was a bunch of us around in Billy's flat. We crushed a load of the tablets down and set up a bit of an auld shooting gallery. The buzz that day was good. The stuff I had was fuckin spot on. Mainlined it, I did, and it blew me bleedin mind. It was only when I was coming down that I noticed Billy sitting there on the sofa, white as a ghost and as still as fuckin death. I jumped up from the floor where I was lying and slapped him across the face a few times. He was still alive, but he was losing it fast.

"Somebody get a fucking ambulance!" I shouted. Everyone knew the pigs would be around soon asking questions, and they all fucked off. I picked Billy up, held him close and tried to waltz some life back into him. We slow-danced about twenty circuits of the living room. Around and around and around. I could feel his body go into spasm and he started to retch. His cheek felt cold and moist propped up against mine. I held him at arm's length to check whether any life was coming back to his face. It was still white. There was vomit running from both sides of his mouth and his eyes were just, well, lifeless.

"Come on, Billy," I cried on his shoulder, "don't die, you bastard.

Don't die, you fucking bastard." I held him close again, dancing, dancing, dancing, around and around and around. I felt puke spill down me back. His body was getting heavier and heavier. "Ambulance'll be here in a minute, Billy. You're gonna be okay," I said, without any conviction at all. The strength was draining out of me too. It was like I was holding a two-kilo bag of potatoes at arm's length and the longer it went on, the worse the pain got. Finally, we both collapsed into a heap on the floor. I didn't need to look at his face again. I knew he was dead –*You did fuck-all for him, ye cunt* –

I remember hearing the sound of sirens approaching. Someone must have called an ambulance. It was too late for Billy, but. The time to look after number one had arrived –*Run, run, ye fuckin coward, ye!* – No, I'd done me best for him, gone way beyond the call of duty to try to save his life. He wasn't even a friend of mine anyway. There are no friends in this game. That's what they say. No friends, just other fuck-ups with the same needs as you. And most of the other cunts Billy knows would have robbed his smack, dipped his pockets and left him to die, instead of doing what I did. My conscience is– it's clear, right?

Or–

Fuck off, I didn't force him to take the stuff. It was his own decision. You make your own choices and you live with it. I never forced him to take it – *Every man for himself. You'll soon have the chance to apologise to him personally* – No, I'm not going to die. Just a bad trip –*It's over. This is the end* –

Stop. Stop now. I'm not going to die. Concentrate on ... Concentrate on The Eagles. Yeh, I love The Eagles ... *Hotel California* ... Hang on, why didn't Redser want to give me his duvet? The bollix. Bet he wanted me to get caught. Supposed to be me mate and all ... No mates in here ... Bet he's down there now, ratting on me, telling all the screws I've had a bad trip. I'll lose me fuckin parole and all over that cunt ...

Enough. It's time for me to sort meself out. Get out of here. Get clean. Get a job. Sort me life out in three steps ... One, Two, Three ... *the Hotel California ... a lovely place* ... Get a bit of auld work and get the few bob together ... Sure, dee don't want to work dese days. Everytings handed to dem on a plate. Dese young ones is havin dese babbies for de money. And who's payin for it? Us ... Have anudder ginger snap, Father ... Sure aren't we a great little country, all the same. We gave more money to Live Aid per person dan any udder country in de world, so we did. Great country ... Don't talk to me about St Vincent de Paul. Sure, that's all new stuff dey're giving out to the so-called poo-er. New washing machines, new cookers, new fridges. Handed to dem on a plate ... Great little nation. Three Eurovisions in a row. No-one else has ever done it ... Irish supporters, best in de world ... Dublin people, salt of de eart ... Gotta get out ... Have a choice ... Billy. Didn't force you. You bought the stuff yourself. You brought it all upon yourself. Tried to help you ... Fires of hell. Damnation–

"Are y'all right, are ye?"

"Who's that?"

"It's me."

"Billy? Is that you, Billy. Oh fuck, Billy, I'm so sorry. I tried to save you. Took the stuff yourself. Nobody forced you to–"

"Who the fuck's Billy? It's me, Redser."

"No, it's not. It's you, Billy, pretending to be Redser."

"Will you shut up ta fuck. It's me, right?"

"Redser?"

"Yeh, it's me. How're ye, y'all right?"

"I'm in the fuckin horrors, man. Is rec over?"

"Just a minute ago. Listen, I covered up for you. The screws asked me where you were and I'm after telling them you'd a headache. They believed me."

"Sound ... Redser?"

"Yeh?"

"I hate this place."

"The Joy?"

"Dublin. Fucking Ireland ... When I get out, I'm leaving."

"Where're you gonna go?"

"California."

"California?"

"Such a lovely place ... lovely place."

"Sure it is. Are you gonna be all right?"

"I'm not sure. I'm in a fuckin heap, man."

"Try and get a night's sleep."

"Listen, Redser. Thanks, right?"

"No problem. I'm just here if you need me. If you wake up in the middle of the night, just wake me up as well. But try and get some sleep, right?"

◆　　◆　　◆

HEALTHY BODY, UNHEALTHY MIND

A fit body is a healthy body. That's my motto. It hasn't always been. The abscesses and track marks on me arms speak for themselves. But it's never too late to start looking after yourself, though I must admit most of us did have an ulterior motive for being so enthusiastic about the idea of setting up aerobics classes in here. She was blonde, tanned and a vision in purple lycra. While it's true that, after years inside, even Ethel out of "EastEnders" would be enough to get most of the sex-starved bastards in here aroused, this bird who came in to tell us about the aerobics was quite definitely an authentic, 24-carat gold stunner.

And while we went along to the first meeting to have a laugh at the idea of trying to introduce physical fitness to The Joy, we were suddenly talking about developing parts of our bodies we couldn't pronounce before and toning up muscles we never knew existed. Our memories of this woman and the thought of watching her shapely body bouncing about in front of us have kept us going for a week. Now, the day has finally come. Track-suited and lacquered from head to toe in deodorant, we stand around in the gym and wait for her to arrive. It must be said, we look a pack of prize pricks in our t-shirts, which expose our tracks, open sores and Indian ink tattoos for all to see. Her expectations hopefully won't be high. You can't knock us for trying, but.

She arrives in. This bird is class. She has a ghetto blaster with her. She is as beautiful, and probably more beautiful, than any of us remembered her. "Ever tried doing aerobics with a horn on ye?" one of the lads says. Everyone laughs. Except me. I've fallen in love with her and I resent the lads talking about her like she's some sort of sex object.

There is another woman with her. A small, plump woman in her fifties, I'd say, who could do with losing a bit herself. We decide she must be some kind of registrar. "Don't fancy yours much," I say. Everyone laughs again. Then we start jockeying for position at the front of the gym, all of us anxious to get the best view possible of the supermodel.

She's a beaut, no doubt about it. She's wearing this blue sweatshirt with a white t-shirt underneath, white runners and grey cotton tracksuit bottoms which are so tight she must have had to grease her legs to get the things on. Though I'm not a sexist arsehole like the rest of the blokes in here, I have to admit I'm looking forward to watching her bending down in those. The comment about the hard-on is playing on me mind. I'm sending telepathic signals downwards, ordering me lad to behave himself. If it starts trying to burrow its way out of me tracksuit bottoms, then I'll never live it down.

"Can we have silence, everybody?" the supermodel says, her voice sounding even sexier than it had the first time.

Silence? You can have anything you want, ye stunner, ye.

"Okay, can we keep it down."

No, I'm doing me best, but I don't think I can.

"Quiet!" And there was quiet. "Now, are you all looking forward to your aerobics workout today?"

Stupid question. Do men piss on the floor in public toilets? There's a loud "Yeh!" from everyone.

"Good," she says.

And then she breaks it to us. "This lady here with me today is your aerobics instructor."

No. Couldn't be. There's quiet now all right. Silence. Disbelief. Complete deflation. We've been suckered.

"I hope you'll all be nice to her."

The screws are breaking their shites laughing. The supermodel whispers her last words of encouragement to her mate and then she says goodbye to us. I think about running after her, to tell her how I feel, like, but I don't. Yer one introduces herself. We try to remain as upbeat as possible, though, as she turns on the music and runs us through some basic moves. "Left, left, left ... and switch ... and right, right, right ... and switch ..."

Downhearted or not, we pick it up quickly. "Left, left, left ... and switch ... and right, right, right ... and switch ..."

"Hands in the air now!" she shouts. She's fitter than we thought. "Up, One, Two, Three and Down, One, Two, Three ..."

Someone up the front has the giggles and soon it ripples down through the rest of the group. Everyone's starting to enjoy themselves now, all seeing the funny side of being taught aerobics by a woman who's twice our age.

"Left, left, left ... and switch ... and right, right, right ... and switch ..." we're all chanting, in between roarin laughter.

"Hang on!" one of the lads shouts out, "Was that two to the left or three?" Watching our own lack of co-ordination makes us laugh even more. Me sides will be sore tomorrow and it won't be from the strain of the exercise.

"Okay, everybody," she says, "everybody bring your hands down and touch your toes."

"Ah, that's it!" someone shouts at the front. "I'm not doing it any more. Touch me toes? I can't even touch me fuckin knees, so I can't."

The woman laughs, fair play to her. "By the time you get out of here, you'll be able to stand on your hands."

I can't see how that's going to prepare us for life on the outside, unless we're all gonna join Fossett's Circus or something. After five minutes, we're all bollixed and we stop. Somehow, I don't think aerobics is going to catch on in here now.

I won't be back. I've had me heart broken today. Once bitten and all that. As I sit on the gym floor, trying to recapture me breath, me sodden t-shirt clinging to me body, I wonder to meself where the supermodel went this afternoon. I'm lovesick. She's probably up in Arbour Hill right now, teaching aerobics to the rapists and sex offenders. I'm thinking of writing a letter to me TD.

♦   ♦   ♦

85

UNFINISHED LETTERS

Dear Martina,

I've been wanting to write to you for ages, but I just didn't know how. I'm not even sure if you remember who I am. I've been sitting here in my cell for hours, trying to think up a way to start this letter and there's about twenty screwed-up pieces of paper on the floor, where I've started one, read it back, thought it sounded stupid, crumpled it up and thrown it away.

Martina, there's no other way to say this, so I'm just going to say it straight out. I still love you. My mates all say I'm mad writing to you or even having anything at all to do with you after you did the dirt on me with Rat Boy, but the truth is I can't stop thinking about you. That's not the gargle or the drugs talking, Martina. And I'm not only saying it because I'm in here.

I know it's been a while with no contact at all. No letters or calls or visits or nothing. I don't even know if you're still living in the flat, though Duffo said he saw you up there a couple of months back, so I'm just presuming you are. I heard all about you and Rat Boy breaking up and I was really sorry to hear it. Really I was. But I think it's for the best, because you two aren't meant to be together. We are though. Me and you. Remember all the laughs we used to have? We did everything together, didn't we? Things can be the same again. I know they can.

The thing is, I blamed you for what happened with Rat Boy, but all along I knew it was my fault. I have to swallow my pride and say that. If I hadn't been so into the gear and the robbing, then I'd never have been sent away and you would never have had to look to another man to show you the love you needed. I understand that. But I'm after getting off the gear now. I'm not using anymore and I'll never be using again. I've finished with all that shite. I promise you. Martina, please come and see me. I'm begging you. I've nothing in my life in here. I've nothing to look forward to. Even when I get out.

If you even wrote to me or came to see me, then I'd have something to cling to. A dream. Something to believe in. I've only about a few months of this sentence left and you never know, I might even be out by the end of the summer if I keep out of trouble. Think of that. We could be making a new start together. Me, you and the kid.

But first, I just want the truth, Martina. I don't understand why you had to tell me ma and da they were going to be grandparents and then just walk away and not tell them whether they really were or whether it was all a load of bollix. You hurt us all, you lying cow. And you always blamed me for everything. For robbing and getting put inside. You bitch. Why did ...

ALIVE AND KICKING

Boyo gets what he deserves, everyone agrees. He's fair game. There's open season in here on cunts who did what he did. He's not just a normal rapist. He raped auld ones and kids as well. He is hated, even among the other jockeys, which is what I find incredible. Take the Hulk, for example. He's a right bastard. One of those meat-headed gym freaks, who spends hours lifting weights because he thinks it makes him more of a man. He's a rapist himself. He did some really terrible things to birds. But whether it's because Boyo is a knacker who dared to do it to members of the settled community or whether it's because he chose such easy targets, the Hulk's always going on about what he's going to do to him if he ever finds himself alone with him and a blade in a cell. "Where's that little faggot?" he walks around the place shouting whenever he's in a bad mood. "Tell that little queer fucker I'm gonna kill him."

It's all a load of shite to me. This idea that if it's straight rape, it's all right, but if you do it to auld ones or little boys, you're scum. To me, all jockeys are scum. I've done a lot of things in me life that I'm ashamed of. But Boyo and the Hulk are no different from each other, they both fucked up people's entire lives just to get their rocks off for a few minutes.

The Hulk's getting a bit of hassle from a couple of the screws at the moment and he's walking around like a fucking maniac, just looking for someone to hit. "Where's that faggot?" he's shouting, as I wander down to collect me lunch. Boyo must be able to hear him, because he's too frightened to leave his cell to go down and get his food. As I pass by his door, I notice it's shut and furniture is being moved around inside. I reckon he must be barricading himself in in case yer man completely loses it and tries to get in at him.

As I start buttering me bread roll up in me cell, this loud scream pierces the air down the landing. It's Boyo all right. Fuckin definite. The Hulk is in his cell. That noise I heard earlier must have been him pushing Boyo's bed and table up against the door before he started beating him. That way when the screws come to answer Boyo's screams for help, the Hulk'll have an extra ten seconds or so to cause the poor fuck a bit more serious damage. Boyo must be getting a heavy bating, because I've hardly ever heard him scream this loud, even that time when they held him down and poured scalding water over his body. Stupid cunt didn't even report that. Never does. Doesn't want to be a grass, which would give the boys another excuse to bate him.

Then the screaming stops, as abruptly as it started. The Hulk slips out of the cell before the kickers arrive. They burst in to find Boyo with a bedsheet wound round his neck and the other end tied to the window. The Hulk'd tried to hang him. Out on the landing, he's ranting to us about how he's done society a favour by killing the little queer and we're all wondering whether he's really murdered him. As

88

we go down for our dinner, there's talk of nothing else. The screws tell us that Boyo is alive, but only just. He had been beaten half-unconscious anyway. It was lucky for him they found him before he choked to death. He lives to fight another day. Maybe that should be *un*lucky for him.

◆　◆　◆

A CRY FOR HELP

I can't even remember what I was supposed to have said. Out of me head I was at the time, so I just have to take their word for it that I made some derogatory remark about the sexual habits of one of the screw's mothers. Insulting people's auld ones is a tactic I often use in arguments, so the likelihood is I'm guilty as charged. But whatever I said, they've no right to take away me books. They're after banning me from the library for three weeks and the petty bastard screws are conducting daily searches of me cell to make sure none of the lads are slipping me in the odd paperback. Three Freddie Forsythes and a couple of Harold Robbins they've taken off me so far. Sixteen hours a day I spend in this fuckin cell, on me own or with some other cunt if they decide to move someone in. With the help of the sleeping pills they give you in here – all in liquid form – I'll sleep for six or seven of those hours. What the fuck do they expect me to do for the other nine or ten? With no bleedin books. Cunts. I'm supposed to just lie here on me bed all day staring at the fucking ceiling. Nothing to do but think, especially about the cruelty of letting a bloke get three quarters of the way through *The Fourth Protocol* and then taking it off him.

I start to think about me days in Pat's, when I used to look out a window just like this and scope all the birds in the yard. Not much to look at, mind you, but when you're eighteen and locked up you'd get up on anything. Except for those three wagons who we used to call the Barking Dogs. Fat fuckin Sumo wrestlers, they were. They used to do this strip-tease thing for us, pulling their bras down and massaging their tits, licking their lips and rubbing their fannies while they danced round the place. How any of the lads could get turned on by the show I'll never fuckin figure. But every day, I'd hear the blokes in the cells all around me, groaning and shouting curses as they wanked themselves off watching the girls perform.

Brendan Behan must have been rightly locked when he said that he wouldn't mind dwelling in the female prison, if the birds back then were anything like they are now. Thinking about them is making me ill, so I lie back on me bed again, fix me stare on a point on the ceiling and start thinking. How did I get here? It was a shop. No, it was an off-licence. I was strung out, so sick with the withdrawal that I'd have killed. No doubt about it. Knifed any cunt who tried to get in me way. Three of us did the jumpover, me holding a blade up to the bloke's throat while the other two dropped the till on the floor to smash it open. They gathered up all the notes and we bet off in a car we were after robbing down near Christ Church. The bloke recognised us as the lads who'd done his shop before and was able to add enough details to the descriptions he'd given a few weeks earlier to put the Old Bill on to our case. Five years, I got. Piece of piss, Rat Boy told me when I came in. He would say that. He was coming towards the end of a four-stretch for a load of handbag snatches. It flew, according to him. That's why I'm back on the gear again. Just the odd bit though, to see me through.

Me time's not flying. Redser's out at the moment and I'm lonely. I'm depressed. And for the first time since I went down, I'm thinking about how life is passing me by. There's nothing I can do to get back all the time I've spent in this shit-hole. I'm twenty-fuckin-six. There's a whole world beyond these walls. Things are happening. People are falling in love. Getting jobs. Mowing lawns. Learning to drive. Going on holidays. Making home brew. Having babbies. Going to discos.

Bollix, I'm pissed off. Up at quarter past eight to slop out. Wash. Shave. Dress. Breakfast. Back to me fuckin cell. Out again for work. If you're lucky enough to get work in here. Typical. Can't get a job outside, can't get a job inside. Play pool instead. Score some hash. Back to me cell for dinner. Locked up again. Out again. For two hours. More pool. Or fuckin table tennis. Join the card school. Get your tea. Fuckin chicken again. Back to your cell. Telly from five till seven. Then back in me little fuckin peter till one of those cunts wakes me again in the morning to tell me to empty me piss and shit into the toilet down the landing. Oh, the days are just so fuckin full, man.

I started saving up sleeping pills about three weeks ago. They're easy enough to buy off the lads in here and I've been keeping them in me mug, which is about a quarter-full with cold tea. Every few days, I top it up with a bit of hot Rosy to try to dissolve the capsules. If me calculations are right, there are now twenty-two Dalmane 30mg tablets, either fully dissolved or half-melted in the dregs at the end of me mug. It's hardly enough to kill me, but it's enough to get me out to the hospital. Enough to convince the screws that I'm suicidal. Enough to get me to see the shrink. Maybe some bleeding-heart psychiatrist will convince them to let me out. I don't care. I just need someone to talk to.

I pick up the mug and swirl the liquid round and round. The smell off it is woeful. The milk has soured and has formed a white, furry scum on the surface, like froth on the top of a flat pint of Bud. Three or four black and grey capsules, which won't break up, poke their heads out through it. Maybe this stuff will kill me after all. I fill the cup up to the top with water, count to three in me mind and knock the whole thing back. It tastes cold and salty. Some of it runs down me face. I go into a fit of coughing as two capsules stick in me throat. After thirty seconds of gagging, I manage to dislodge them and spit them into me hand. But they slide down well with another little sup of water, which also washes the powdery residue off me gums and the inside of me cheeks. I lie down on me bed and wait for them to take effect.

A screw who has probably heard me coughing opens me door. I'm too drowsy to make out what he says, but he seems to have satisfied himself that I'm all right and he fucks off. The room is spinning. Round and round it goes. I'm wondering to meself how I'm going to let them know that I'm OD-ing now. I know I don't have the strength to get up off the bed. Suddenly, the door is right in front of me and I'm standing up. I give it a quick boot. Next thing I know, I'm back on me bed again, lying on me belly with me hand over me mouth to stop meself puking, wondering to meself whether I really got up and kicked the door or whether I dreamt or imagined it. Wishful thinking, like. Next thing I know, there's a screw standing over me and he's repeating something over and over again. I think it's me name. Twisting me head round, I can just about make out the outline of him. I think I can hear him ask me what's wrong with me. I don't know how I get up the strength to tell him. "I'm after taking a load of sleepers."

All fucking hell breaks loose. There's a load of shouting and that going on and the screw's slapping me on the face, picking me up and slow-dancing me round the cell, as if I'm not dizzy enough. When we stop, I fall down on to the cold floor on me hands and knees. Me stomach throws up this flood of baby sick, which splatters across the floor, all over the screw's rhythm and blues and up his trouser legs. There's this long, saliva tightrope left hanging between me mouth and his shoes which breaks as I lift up me head and see a group of people arrive. One of them's firing off questions at me, so I reckon he's a doctor, though me eyes are too heavy to open so I can check this. I feel a hard slap across me face. Then a second one, which is even harder.

I manage to wrench me eyelids open and notice that I'm lying on a stretcher now and I'm moving at a rapid pace, with all these guys running beside me. The screw whose shoes I puked on must be the one dealing out the slaps, because he's shouting at me: "What did you take? What did you take?"

"Just a few sleepers," I groan. Me stomach heaves again.

"How many?" He slaps me again. "How many did you take?"

"About twenty or so," I say, turning me head away. Me left cheek is stinging like fuck at this stage.

"Did you drink anything with them?" he asks.

"Just some tea." The shutters go down on me eyes again.

"Keep talking to him," I hear another voice shout in front of me. "Keep talking to him. Don't let him go to sleep."

I tear me eyes open before anyone has a chance to hit me again.

"Why did you do it?" the screw asks me.

"Dunno."

"Have you any problems at home?"

I shake me head.

"Is anyone in your family on the gear?" he asks.

I don't answer.

"Have you been to see the psychiatrist lately? Have you? Come on. Come on, wake up. Have you been to see the psychiatrist lately?"

I shake my head, vehemently enough for him to fuck off asking me questions. Next thing I know, I'm lying on a trolley and a doctor's massaging me neck and talking to me. The same bleeding questions as before, but I'm better disposed towards him. "No, I've no problems at home," I tell him.

Then the cunt says the magic words, "Let's pump him out." New life is suddenly breathed into me. The thing is, I've been pumped out once before, when I collapsed after a cocktail of smack, tablets and gargle in the middle of the street. Some prick of a good citizen brought me to Pearse Street and an experience that still gives me nightmares to this day. Goosebumps appear on the back of me neck whenever I think about the feeling of that tube being lowered down me throat and the bastarding doctors hoovering me stomach out.

"Wait," I say to the doctor. "You don't need ... to pump me out. I only had twenty-odd and I'm ... already ... after getting sick." The doctor looks at me thoughtfully, but buys me story.

It's difficult to tell whether it's morning or evening when I wake up. It must be morning, though, because the bloke in the bed opposite is gnawing at a Weetabix that's balanced on his spoon. A nurse asks me whether I fancy any breakfast, but I still feel a bit Moby, so I say no. I stare at the ceiling until someone else comes and asks whether I want to see the psychiatrist. I do.

The shrink is just like I expected him to be. Just your average well-meaning, suburban, heavily mortgaged, casually but expensively dressed head-shrinker. Sitting there with this trying-to-look-important-but-not-too-condescending face, the cunt. His opening gambit is just as predictable as his fuckin appearance. "Why did you feel the urge to try to kill yourself?"

I shrug. "Dunno, Doctor."

"Dave," he says, smiling warmly. "Call me Dave."

I think I prefer "Doctor". It's obviously some tactic the cunts are taught to get you to open up. I start to tell the fucker what he wants to hear. "Dave, I just don't know what came over me."

"Well, let's try to find out, shall we? Was it a family matter perhaps?"

"A family matter?"

"Yes. Perhaps there are problems at home that are causing you anxiety?"

I think about me ma and da and their reaction when they found out their youngest son, the one who cried whenever he saw a needle as a boy, had grown up to be an armed robber with a £60-a-day junk habit.

"No, Dave," I tell him, shaking me head. "No problems at all at home."

"No arguments, tensions, anything like that?"

"None at all. Me family come up and see me every week and it's great, like. No arguments or nothin."

"How long have you left to serve of your sentence?"

"Ah, years. I'm only after coming in for five."

"And is that causing you anxiety then? Unhappiness? Perhaps you feel suicidal when you think about the future and how much time you have left to serve."

"It's not that. It's not the future, right? It's now. You know. I'm in here, rotting away and no-one gives a fuck, right? And I know the stuff I did was wrong and I'm paying me debt to society and all that bollix, right? But this is the way I feel. Nothing's standing still for me out there. By the time I get out, everything will have changed. Life's going on. It's passing me by. Things are happening that I should be part of, but I'm not. It's a waste. It's all a fuckin waste, man."

"Good. This is good."

"I'm sorry, Dave."

"No, no. Don't apologise. It's very healthy to let your anger out. Don't turn it in. That's what causes depression – when you suppress your feelings. What kind of things do you feel are passing you by?

What do you feel you are missing out on?"

"Sometimes ..."

"Yes?"

"Sometimes, I just wish I was settled, Dave, you know. Like you."

"You mean married, perhaps, with children, nice house, good job. That kind of thing?"

"Yeh," I tell him. I don't know why I said that. I don't know why I led him down this avenue at all. Perhaps using the cunt's Christian name like I am has me telling him the sort of stuff I reckon he'd like to hear. "Wife, house, kids and job. That'd sort me out. Does that sound stupid?"

He has a really understanding look on his face. It's fucking annoying me. "It doesn't sound stupid at all."

There's a long pause before his next question. "Are you taking any drugs at the moment, other than prescribed medication?"

"The odd bit of smack. Not sure if that counts."

"You're taking heroin?"

"Ah no, I'm not addicted or nothin. Sure, I was off it a while back, you know? Just a couple of turn-ons a week is all I'm getting in, just to help me through and that."

"Are you telling me if you weren't in here at the moment, you wouldn't be taking drugs at all?"

"'Course I wouldn't."

"Well, you didn't start taking heroin in here, I presume?"

"No, that was years ago."

"Can I ask you why you started taking heroin in the first place? A lot of people who take heroin have low self-esteem when they're younger. Did you have problems at school, with your schoolwork maybe, an inability to keep up with the rest of the class? Perhaps you were inhibited socially? Or easily led? Or maybe you–"

"Look," I interrupt him. "It was nothing like that, right? Someone just offered it to me one day and I took it. I didn't like it much, but the lads all said it got better and I was curious. So I took it a few more times and I started to like it. No, I loved it. Yeh, loved it ... Have you ever tried it, have ye?"

"No, I haven't."

"Right, well, it's like an orgasm, man. Like every bit of your body having an orgasm. And it went from being an important part of my life to the most important part and after a while the only important part. Got to the stage where nothing else mattered to me. It was just, we all knew there was fuck-all out there for us. A big black hole of fucking nothingness. And we thought ..."

"Yes?"

"We thought everyone else and everything else was boring as fuck, right? You know, we'd watch them, going out to do a day's work at eight o'clock in the morning, when we were only heading off to the Margaret for the day."

"The Margaret?"

"The Margaret Thatcher. The scratcher."

"Oh, the bed. I see."

"Anyway, fuck all that, we said. Fuck bosses and career ladders and stress and kissing some suit's arse every day just to try to add an extra few bob on to your salary by the end of the decade. Know what I mean?"

"But wouldn't you settle for that now?"

"No."

He looks confused. I'm tying the bloke in knots. "But I thought you said you wanted to settle down. You said earlier you wanted a job, a wife, a house, children."

"No ... What I meant was – all right, I lied. Right? I couldn't give a fuck about houses and mortgages and residents' association meetings. Wives and arguments. Kids and fucking school books and new shoes. I couldn't cope with that shit. All's I have to worry about in me life right now is where me next turn-on is coming from."

"Can I ask you, do you really feel suicidal?"

"No, I feel down. I feel ... Or I felt ... I just need to get me head straight, right?"

I stand up to leave. "It's being in here that's doing it to me. It's got nothing to do with me family, the gear, me childhood, me education. You spend a couple of nights in The Joy and I promise you you'll need something a bit stronger than tranks to get you through the day."

Before too long, I'm back in me cell again. Getting all that stuff off me chest really helped. I feel better now. There's a lot I have to be grateful about. Tomorrow morning, I get me privileges back and I can't wait to find out what happens at the end of *The Fourth Protocol*. I can hear shouting from the cell next door, me neighbour must be enjoying a good wank. Maybe he's a former borstal boy, like me, thinking about the Barking Dogs. Just shows, fuck-all changes round here.

◆　◆　◆

REFLECTIONS: JAMES BOND AND BRISTLE-HEAD

Usually, I was a shrewd enough judge of character, but I totally misjudged that Doctor Kananga fella. Fair enough, he had his faults but he wasn't all bad. He was after telling that James Bond about his master plan to cultivate these massive poppy plantations on his island down in the Caribbean, manufacture a couple of million tons of smack and then give it away free of charge to people in America. The unfortunate downside of Doctor Kananga's plan was that fifty or sixty million Americans would have become addicts by the time all the free gear ran out and then they'd be expected to buy it off him. All right, it wasn't exactly infallible, right? But a welfare state for junkies is a great idea. If Charlie Haughey or Garret FitzGerald had had that kind of foresight, then most of us would never have been locked up in the first place.

I was alone in me support for him, though. The other lads in the borstal with me – servile bastards that they were – had fallen for auld Roger Moore's death-defying heroism, Brylcreamed slickness, repertoire of sickening chat-up lines and the watch that Q was after giving him with the hyper-intensified magnetic field powerful enough to deflect a bullet at long range. The roar that went up when he used it to unzip the back of some bird's dress was deafening. "Sheer magnetism," the smarmy bastard said, raising one eyebrow. All the boys laughed. Cunts.

Not me, though. See, I'm more broad-minded than that. Prepared to see both sides of an argument, to consider the possibility that maybe Doctor Kananga has his heart in the right place after all.

The Big Movie Night was one of the few things that made the teenage years we spent in Pat's bearable. This particular night, though, I had one eye on *Live and Let Die* and the other on Squirrel, who was sitting beside me. Squirrel was a messer who was guaranteed to get you into trouble if you went anywhere near him. Forget any of the gadgetry you've ever seen Bond get off Q. Squirrel was a bastard for throwing the ping-pong smoke bomb and I was sitting next to him the first night he detonated the fuckin thing. He had a table tennis ball in his hand, burned a small hole in it with the tip of a cigarette and spent the first twenty minutes of the film blowing smoke into the opening, which he then covered over with his thumb. Just before the heat perished the plastic, he dropped the ball in the aisle and stamped on it. There was a loud bang, a huge cloud of white smoke and all hell broke loose. I'd avoided sitting near him ever since, but this was the only seat available when I arrived this night, so I didn't have the luxury of choice. I tried not to become too engrossed in the film, though.

I couldn't believe it. Doctor Kananga was after catching Bond rapid torching his poppy fields and he had the chance to kill him. I wouldn't have shed any tears. But it always beats the shit out of me why the baddies in the Bond movies always insist on over-elaborating his killing. Like all supporters of Doctor Kananga's free smack scheme, I would have liked to see him shoot Roger Moore in the face there and then. Instead, what did he do? He slashed Bond's wrist, tied him to a cage with that Jane Seymour bird and tried to lower them into a pool of sharks.

Anyway, this provided me with a distraction I would later regret. Something was burning. I could smell it. I looked down and couldn't believe me eyes. That culchie lad who came in this morning was sitting in front of me with the tail of his shirt on fire and Squirrel was slipping a lighter into his pocket and smirking at me. I let out this yelp and Squirrel jumped to his feet. "Your shirt's on fire," he shouted in the bloke's ear. "Get it off ye quick!" The culchie started screaming. The flames were licking up his back, as he tore his shirt open and threw it on the ground in one quick movement. "Officer! Officer!" Squirrel shouted. "Come quick. Look what's after happening to the fella's shirt."

He was a devious bastard, no doubt about it. By drawing attention to it himself, he knew that suspicion would be slow to fall on him. He was so cool. It struck me that he would have made a bloody good Bond himself, were it not for the fact that the only Bond that mattered to either of us when we were young fellas was the Oliver Bond, where we used to go to score the odd time. But if Squirrel had gone to drama classes instead of spending his evenings casing gaffs, perfecting handbrake turns in stolen cars and developing an unhealthy appetite for palf and gee-gees, then he might have been up there on the screen himself. He just took a wrong turn at a badly signposted intersection on the uphill road that is life, as me auld mate Father Cleary might have said.

Anyway, fuck Squirrel. Because while he was playing the innocent, the spotlight was going to fall on me, seeing as I was the one sitting directly behind the culchie when his shirt went up. By the time the screws arrived over, the shirt was just a smoking lump of charred material on the floor, but the culchie was still in shock and still dancing around the place like he was having an eppo. The lights were turned on, which didn't go down well with the rest of the lads at all. They missed the bit where Bond cuts through the ropes tying his hands, drags Doctor Kananga into the shark pool and shoves a high pressure bullet into his mouth, which blows him up and bursts him like a beach ball. "We're missin it, turn the fuckin lights back off!" everyone's shouting.

"It's that fuckin culchie," someone said. "Trouble-making bastard. Shoulda just taken the shirt off and stamped it out on the ground, 'stead of callin over the screws and ruinin the film for everyone."

They all knew, though, that the show was over for the night and made do with putting their hands in front of the projector light to make bunny shadows on the screen. Squirrel, meantime, was beginning to sound like The Sweeney on speed, cross-examining everyone in the room: "Did you see anything, did you? Don't give me that, you must have, you're only sitting a few feet away from him."

Squirrel was blowing it, because the two of us were getting fierce looks off one of the screws. He pointed at the two of us. "Don't move youse," he said. "Stay behind afterwards."

When the rest of the lads had gone, he asked us which one of us had done it. "Wasn't me," said Squirrel, "and it wasn't him either. I was sitting beside him. I'd have seen him ... Might have been someone down the back, though. They were throwing oranges all bleedin night. I'm after getting hit I don't know how many times. Jaysus, comes to something when you can't even watch a film in peace in this place."

"Quiet," the screw shouted. We didn't argue after that. He told us we were both being put on report and we were sent back up to our landing for the night, only to guess what our punishment would be the next morning. I didn't sleep well that night, because Squirrel kept banging on me wall and shouting in to me from next door. "What d'ya think's gonna happen to us in the morning?"

"Nothing's gonna happen to me, 'cos I'm gonna tell them it was you," I told him, just trying to put the shits up him, like.

"You can't do that, man."

"I can and I'm gonna. I'm sick of it, Squirrel, and so are the rest of the lads. We can't even watch a film now, but you're ruinin it for everyone. So that's it. I'm not changing me mind. I'm gonna tell them it was you in the morning."

He must have been bricking himself all night, because he had that look about him the next morning, as though he'd had no sleep. I was after emptying me piss-pot into the jacks when he walked in. "You're not gonna grass me really, are ye?" he asked.

"'Course I am," I said. I somehow managed to keep a straight face. "No way I'm taking the rap for you, Squirrel. I've only a few weeks of me sentence left. Trying to keep me nose clean, I am."

He looked at me with these big fuckin puppy dog eyes. "Please, man, don't do it. I've only got a few weeks left."

"You should've thought about that before you did it," I said, as I finished rinsing out me pot in the sink and turned to leave. I can't remember whether I heard the dull-sounding thunk first or felt the blow, but he whacked me hard across the back of the head with his pot. I hit the deck and he was straight on top of me, pucking the face off me and trying to pin me down. I brushed off his grip and kicked him off me with both feet. A crowd of lads, having heard the noise, gathered around the door of the toilets to watch. I lunged at Squirrel, wrapping me two hands around his throat and tried to shove him into one of the toilet booths, where there'd be no room for him to move while I bet the shite out of him. He had the same idea. He caught me full in the face with a punch that opened up me lip and he tried to turn me around. But we both turned right round and we fell forward on to the floor, into a puddle of piss, and I closed the door with me foot. We struggled on the floor together for a few minutes until I freed me hands and hit him a couple of good digs in the head.

Then all of a sudden, somebody hit the door a boot. We stopped fighting and looked around. It was Bristle-Head. A small bloke with bristly hair who was the toughest fuckin screw in the borstal. He just smiled at us and said: "Call that a fuckin fight?"

Me and Squirrel jumped up. "No, we weren't fighting," I said.

"On the contrary," said Squirrel, as subtle as a fucking Roger Moore eyebrow movement. "Sure, we were only havin a bit of a mess."

"That's right, yeh. We were only muckin about, like."

Bristle-Head nodded, laughed and just walked off. Was it any wonder that all the inmates thought so highly of him? He was no ordinary screw, ye see. He wasn't the kind of man who hid behind his authority by putting you on report if you gave him lip or if he caught you fighting. He'd sort it out himself and we respected him for that. He'd say things like: "Let's go into that cell, lock the door and me and you will have it out." Probably wasn't even fuckin serious, but no-one ever took up his challenge. He was a hard bastard.

Me and Squirrel both stood there in the jacks for a few minutes after he left, smiling and shaking our heads, in admiration, like. "Lucky for you he came in when he did," I said to him then.

"Lucky for me? I was battering ye," he said.

"You were in your arse. Look at the state of you, you're in bits, man."

"That's only 'cos you fight like a fucking bird."

I punched him in the face and he hit his head off the wall of the booth and, within seconds, Bristle-Head had arrived back to find us rolling around in the piss again, kicking and spitting and trying to get in the one clean punch that would have finished the fight. "Up!" he shouted at us. "Get up the pair of you."

We stood up. He stared at the two of us for ages, without saying anything. Then he just said: "You wanna fight, then come with me."

He brought us up to this empty cell upstairs and ordered us in. We thought he was going to offer to take the two of us on. "He's a mad bastard," Squirrel whispered to me. "I don't want to fight him. Even if he says he'll take the two of us together, right?"

"Right, lads," Bristle-Head said, when we were inside. "Don't look so scared, I'm not going to hurt you. But I'll lock this door, right? Then you can kill each other if you want. I'll just make sure you're not disturbed."

He closed the door and locked it. Me and Squirrel just sat down on the bed. We never said nothing for ages. Then Squirrel asked: "So what do we do now?"

"We're not gonna have another fight, are we?" I said.

"Well, I don't want another fight. D'you?"

"No."

"Well," he said, "let's just sit here for a few minutes, pretend we had a fight and then come out again."

About ten minutes later, Bristle-Head unlocked the door and stuck his head in. "Anyone dead in there yet?" he said. He was in bits laughing.

Me and Squirrel started breaking our bollix as well. The guy had style, no fucking question about it. All the lads in the borstal felt the same way about him. For some, I think he was the father figure that had been missing from their lives. In all me years inside, Bristle-Head is the most decent human being I have ever come across. I remember he once had all the lads in the borstal down on their hands and knees scrubbing their cell floors with little nailbrushes. He never ordered anyone to do it. He just convinced everyone to take pride in their cells. So there we were, a generation of psychos, pick-pockets, car thieves, junkies, burglars, no-hopers, rent boys and drop-outs, all persuaded that cleanliness was next to godliness. The guy was a fucking genius.

Anyway, the reason I'm reminiscing about him now is that I can see him at this very moment, across the landing. Just like old times, except he's now pacing the landings of The Joy and I'm doing time here. But things aren't as they were, though. Our relationship has changed, you know? I've grown up. Eight years older and I wish I could say wiser. Seeing Bristle-Head now is like bumping into an old school friend on a bus and discovering that, apart from football, you've nothing of passionate interest to say to one another any more. The borstal, to me, was like primary school and The Joy like secondary. Okay, the only real difference between Pat's and The Joy is the age of the guys inside. Otherwise they're both as shitty as each other. But among the prisoners in The Joy, there's an unwritten rule that you're not supposed to fraternise with the screws. They're the enemy. That puts Bristle-Head off limits for an auld heart-to-heart. Even if he's just as he was the first time I met him at the age of eighteen. Who's to say? I just have to maintain this hostility towards him. I'm sure he understands. It's his job after all. Sure, it goes with the salary.

◆　　◆　　◆

TO PROTECT THE PUBLIC

"Do ye want me to do one for ye or wha'?" Duffo's getting a bit pissed off waiting for me to decide, like.

"Much is it?"

He purses his lips and blows hard as he thinks. "Any smack on ye, have ye?"

I shake me head. "Might be getting some in, though. The weekend, maybe?"

He looks at the guy next to him who's rolling down his sleeve and has this real pained expression on his face. Then he looks back at me. "Right," he says, pulling out a needle. "I'll do it for you now. Seeing as we're mates, like."

I'm having second thoughts, but, as the other bloke gets up to leave. "Don't forget," Duffo shouts after him, "ye keep it clean by rubbing disinfectant on it. With a cloth. If it gets infected, then come back to me, right? You'll be sorted."

He's unscrewing the lid off a jar of green ink when I decide to back out. "Listen, I, em, I think I'll, ye know, give it an auld miss."

But he gets a bit aggro. Like he's really offended. "Ye fuckin shiter, ye. Not trust me, do ye not? Don't worry about all this Aids shite. Sure, I'm after cleaning the needle and everything. Sit down, man."

"Nah, listen, thanks all the same, but. I don't really want one anyway. No offence, like."

"Right," Duffo says, like he's deeply hurt. "Don't change your fuckin mind now, 'cos you won't be getting one off of me."

The thing is, I'm not scared at all. Needles don't frighten me. Not any more. Duffo should know that better than anyone, seeing as he was the bloke who introduced me to the gear in the first place. The real reason is that he wouldn't be able to draw the kind of fancy design I'm after. He's just not good enough. He'd chance his arm right

enough – or rather mine – but he'd make a complete dog's bollix of it.
If it's the letters I, R and A you want tattooed across your knuckles,
or if you're wanting a heart with your initials or your ma's and da's
names on your forearm, then Duffo's your man. Then again, if you
wanted something like that, you could feck a jar of ink from the work-
shop yourself and keep your money or smack in your pocket. If I'm
getting one at all, right, I'll get Terry to do it. His are art, man. Pure
fuckin art.

"Chicken shit!" Duffo shouts as I leave his cell.

There's a fat bloke I don't recognise on the other side of our landing. A fat, balding bloke with this thick strand of hair which seems to
stand up all on its own. Fuckin stupid he looks. "Who's that?" I ask
Redser.

He starts laughing. "That's the General. Don't forget to salute
him."

"Me bollix, it's the General."

"It is," he says.

I don't recognise him, but then again I've never seen him before.
He always goes around on the outside with his hand over his face or
wearing the balaclava. When he turns around, though, I can see the
Mickey Mouse t-shirt he was wearing in today's paper. These guys,
like the Viper and the Dunnes, are treated like fuckin gods in here.
Bow to them and kiss their arses, the guys do. When the Viper was in,
sure everyone used to go silent when he'd walk into the gym, which is
where he spent most of his spare time. The General's in on remand,
which is kind of strange, 'cos he's over on our wing along with all
these convicted criminals. Anyway, fuck him and the rest of them. I
won't be doing any brown-nosing. He wouldn't mix with us junkies.
So I'll stay out of his way if he'll stay out of mine. As I stare over at
him, he catches me eye and I scurry off back to me cell.

I've gone mad into the oranges. You can never get too much

Vitamin C, that's what I say. This one I have in me hand came over the prison wall this morning and I managed to sneak it in. It's no ordinary orange, though. It's very special.

I pick it up and start to examine it closely around the stem bit. I find the pin-hole quite easily and, when I press me finger into the peel, a little bit of brown liquid bubbles to the surface. I stick me works into it and draw some of the smack out. What I actually get into the syringe is part smack and part juice, but the orange doesn't matter a fuck because we often use it to purify the gear anyway or to help dissolve it.

I sit down on the floor, with me back against the wall and me legs spread out wide. I'm having a bit of difficulty these days finding new veins to shoot into and have to tourniquet me arm to get one up. So much for me great wiring. I twist up me sheet and wrap it round the top of me arm, holding one end firmly under me armpit and putting the other in me mouth and pulling it tight. I flex me arm up and down a few times and tap hard on it with the tips of me fingers. There's two beauties to choose from. I pick the biggest and bluest. I pierce it with the needle and hesitate for a second before drawing back and then slamming the lot into me.

I fall onto me side. The rush is instant. It's good too, but it's over quick. I enjoy it while it lasts, but. I love oranges. I love everyone.

♦ ♦ ♦

UNFINISHED LETTERS

Dear Martina,

Bad news. I'm back on the gear again. I was off it there for a while. I'm grand though. Not strung out or nothing. Just two or three turn-ons a week is all I'm getting, just to get me through the rest of my sentence. I think it's impossible to stay off the heroin when you're locked up for sixteen hours a day in a cell with no-one to talk to and nothing to talk about even if you did have some-one to talk to. Anyway, this place is a nuthouse. There's some really scary people in here. Three months off it I was, which is my longest ever. But sure, the only reason I went off it was to prove that I could do it when I got out and now I know I can.

So how's it going? I hope you're all right. And the kid as well. I don't even know if it's a boy or a girl. I know we haven't spoken to each other for years, but you don't know what a letter from you would mean to me. Let's forget about the past. I don't want to know about what happened and what didn't happen. Just the future. Is there any chance, Martina? Is there any chance of us getting back together? Please write back to me and say yes. I'm begging you.

Things aren't too bad at the moment. We're all excited in here about the Ireland match next week. I'm even able to tolerate the screws more now. Maybe it's because I'm getting on a bit. One of them came in tonight and threw me in this morning's Star and a couple of smokes. For nothing like. That's put me in a good mood.

Duffo's dropping me over a turn-on any minute now as well. To-morrow, we're all going to ...

◆　　◆　　◆

GOD SAVES A QUEEN

From the second we heard Masher was coming, there was this feeling in the air that something fuckin dreadful was about to happen. As soon as he arrived, he started asking questions about who the most hated person on the wing was. A psychopath looking for a victim, he was. It wasn't surprising that him and Baldy struck up an instant rapport. Two fucked-up people magnetically drawn to one another and, once we saw that, we knew that someone was in for a heavy bating. Our money was on Queenie, a jockey nobody liked. He knew it himself, because he was refusing to come out to get his dinner. He holed himself up in his cell.

The two lads bade their time. They walked around together the whole time, constantly whispering, like they were making plans, talking about what they were going to do when they got hold of him on his own. I couldn't make eye contact with either of them, because they were in the mood for hurting some cunt and I just didn't want it to be me. I walked around wishing I was invisible. The four-by-twos do their best but they can't watch everyone twenty-four hours a day.

It happened about a week later. Four or five of us were sitting around playing cards when we heard screaming coming from Queenie's cell. We were just silent. All too nervous to say or do anything. There had been such a build-up to this, we knew that whatever they were doing to him in there was terrible.

About ten seconds later, Queenie came running out of his cell bleeding very fuckin heavily by the looks of it. Baldy and Masher came charging out after him, Masher holding a toothbrush blade. Baldy punched Queenie full in the face and his head cracked against the wall. He took him in a headlock and marched him back into the cell, Masher following him excitedly. They closed the door behind them and the screaming started again. It all happened in seconds.

The alarms went off and soon the kickers arrived, with their batons and shields. The two boys had already made their exit. None of us said a word as we sat there, wondering whether this time there was anything left of Queenie for them to save.

◆ ◆ ◆

THE RIGHTEOUS BROTHERS

"Teresa's Gardens," I said, jumping into the front passenger seat. The taxi driver just shot me this right aggressive look, like I was just after massacring his family or something. "Twenty quid up front," he said.

"Twenty quid?"

"Yeh, before I even start the car."

"Why?" I said. I was playing the Wounded Innocent card.

"Because you're going there to score heroin or whatever shit it is you're on. And you junkies always leave us sitting in our cars like spare tools, waiting for yiz to come back. And most of the time, you don't. So if a junkie wants to use my taxi to go cruising fuckin Dublin for drugs, then he pays up front. Right?"

Yeh, right enough, you cranky bastard. At this stage, me stomach hurt when I talked, so I didn't bother arguing with him. I just pulled a crumpled twenty out of me pocket and threw it onto the dashboard without bothering to flatten it out. He didn't even look at it, just pulled out of the rank and pointed the car in the direction of the Gardens. The prickly bastard said nothing to me on the way out either. If this keeps up, I thought to meself, I'd have to consider withdrawing me business from this particular firm.

Using the auld Jo Maxis to go out trying to score is an extravagance, I know, but it's part of junkie culture all over the world. Real junkies don't go cruising the heroin hot spots on foot and they don't take the bus. It's got fuck-all to do with the withdrawal symptoms and the need to get to a certain place in as short a time as possible. It's just that when you've got enough money in your pocket for a turn-on you feel like the wealthiest and most important man in the world, so you travel like a man of means.

As well as that, withdrawal does make you less tolerant of the kind of wankers you have to sit beside on buses, though this taxi driver was doing his best to replicate the effect. I was never so pleased to see the flats in the distance, but, instead of dropping me right outside, he just pulled up outside the Player & Wills factory and told me to get out.

"What's the story?" I asked him.

"Not going any further," he said, totting me fare up on the meter.

"Why not?"

"'Cos the Concerned Parents are out doing their rounds around here. Out looking for youse cunts. You can do what you want with your fuckin life, but you're not putting mine at risk, right?"

He gave me the change from me twenty and didn't seem too optimistic about his chances of getting a tip out of me for his stimulating conversation, the grumpy bollix. As I got out, I felt me body shudder and I doubled over with a cramp. The driver looked at me like I was a piece of dog-shite he'd found caked to the sole of his shoe. He mumbled something about "scumbag druggies killing themselves" and drove off in search of another fare. No doubt, he'd tell them all about the junkie loser he had in the car earlier and how the Government should bring back the birch and hanging and borstals and national service.

Still, I couldn't blame him for not wanting to drop me to the door. The Concerned Parents were turning into hysterical parents, coercing information out of vulnerable, strung-out addicts like meself about dealers and then marching in huge gangs and forcing them to move out of their family homes. They were after shutting down me favourite places for scoring, voluntary liquidation, if you know what I mean. Restraint of trade, I'd call it. I thought it was high time the pigs did something about these people.

The shortcut to the Gardens took me into the grounds of the cigarette factory and then the church. I stood at the railings, from where I could see me dealer and I wolf-whistled him to try to catch his attention. But I also caught the attention of a vigilante night-time patrol. You'd have known them a mile off. They didn't exactly blend into their surroundings, you know. They all had this self-important air about them, with a few nightclub bouncer/store detective types there for muscle. They were all frustrated pigs, these fellas anyway.

Charles Bronson seemed a good name for the one who appointed himself me interrogator. "What the fuck are you doing hanging around here?" he said. "We don't want any of your shit around here, right? So turn around and get the fuck out of here while ye still have legs to carry ye."

"What are you talking about? I'm just cutting through," I said. I was starting to shit meself a bit now.

"Cutting through from where?"

"There," I pointed.

"That's Player & Wills."

"I know it's Player & Wills. I've been hanging around there. You know, just mooching about to see if I could get a few auld smokes and that."

"Don't give me that," Bronson said. "Bleedin place is crawling with security in there. I know what you're mooching about for and it's not smokes. Do I look like an eejit?"

He did, but I said no.

"I've seen you before. I know your face. Now I'm going to tell you for the first and last time. There's no more drugs being sold from these flats, right?"

"I'm not even into the drugs."

"Turn out your pockets," he said, throwing the head with me now.

"Who the bleedin fuck are you? Turn out me pockets?"

"I'm telling ye, turn them out," he said. "Turn them out. If you don't, I'll call the rest of the lads over and we'll all search you instead. Do ye want that?"

They were over like lightning. They just grabbed me, bent me over the railings and frisked me. Bronson fished into the pocket of me wax jacket and pulled out nineteen quid in tattered notes and me works, which he held up to me face. "Just mooching around, looking for a few smokes, eh?" he said, as though it somehow justified the stop-and-search powers the fat bastard had given himself. Without taking his eyes off me, he dropped me syringe and stamped it into the ground.

"I'm sorry to have to do that, but it's for yer own good," he said, as if he suddenly felt pity for me. Well, I thought to meself, I'd rather be a junkie than a fascist prick who pretends to be into community welfare just because he can't get a hard-on without acting out some scene from fucking *Deathwish*.

The thing was, I recognised Bronson then. I remembered that when I was seventeen, I used to score napps, palf and gee-gees off his brother. I was tempted to tell him this. To tell him that if his auld one had had a headache the night his brother was conceived, then I might never have got into the drugs. But his three mates who looked like Rottweilers were straining to be let off their leashes and I knew if I did I'd probably end up crushed into as many pieces as me works.

Bronson squeezed the money back into me hand and told me to go and get maintenance treatment, get meself cleaned up, get a hobby, settle down, get a career, marry a nice girl, have children and live happily ever after. I felt the cramps take hold of me stomach again and the skin-crawling sensation of me shirt sleeves rubbing off me tender, goose-pimpled arms as I turned me back and trudged off in the direction of the bus stop.

♦ ♦ ♦

I'M ABSOLUTELY POSITIVE

How could I have been so stupid? I came to London to try to make a new start for meself, get away from me so-called mates, get off the gear, get an auld job. Old habits die hard though, it's true. I was standing on the kerb in Trafalgar Square, waiting for the little man to turn green, when this bitch pulls up at the lights in a flash car. Me eyes had a mind of their own, man. No matter how much I tried, I couldn't help looking at the handbag on the front passenger seat. I don't even remember deciding to rob the bleedin thing. I just suddenly found meself with a rock in me hand, smashing the fuck out of the window and, while yer one was screaming, grabbing the bag and legging it.

There was fuck-all in it, but the grumpy cunt of a judge I was up in front of refused to take that into account. He did take into account that I was on the run from the law in Ireland for another jumpover I did. Three years he gave me. Three years for a bleedin handbag. That's British justice for you. So now I find meself in one of Her Majesty's prisons for the first time. The atmosphere in here is a lot better than in any Irish prison I've been in, due to the much lower psychopath-to-normal person ratio, but I'd still love to be back in Dublin tonight. There's murder going on there apparently.

All the prisoners who were found to have the virus were shanghaied out to Arbour Hill, where they are being kept in isolation and generally treated like lepers. I've heard stories about screws walking round in there in fuckin spacesuits and serving them up their dinners on paper plates with plastic cutlery and everything. That's bleedin degrading, like. I don't know much about Aids, the virus or whatever you call it, but you don't catch it from fuckin touching someone or drinking out of their cup. So they say, anyway. I thought that stuff went out the window along with all that shite about it being a queer's disease and God's wrath and all that. Paper cups and plates and fuckin plastic knives and forks. Heavy shit, man.

But the Dublin boys are fighting back against narrow-minded ways. A bunch of them have climbed up on the roof of Arbour Hill, with placards and everything. Fair fucks to them.

There's a knock on me door. One of the Irish lads in here has managed to get me a copy of yesterday's paper, so I can read all about it. The screw lets him drop it into me. "Fair fucks to the lads," he says as he hands me it. I sit on me bed and open it out. Big banner headlines. And a photograph. Of the lads on the roof. Jaysus, look who it is. If it isn't me auld mate ...

Oh Jesus Christ ...

This isn't ...

Can't be ...

True ...

There's a rush of blood to me head and me body suddenly feels all cold and numb. I fold the paper up quickly and throw it down onto the bed. I can't look at it. I can't ... The back page catches me eye. Sports, I like sports. Have a look. Have a read. See how your team got on. Villa. Bollix, beaten again ... Sack the board, sack the players, sack the manager. Graham Taylor must go. Bring back Tony Barton, the cunt. Bring back the days when being a Villa fan was something to be proud of. Name the European Cup-winning side of 1982 – Nigel Spink, Des Bremner, Colin Gibson, Ken McNaught, Allan Evans ... em, Tony Morley, yeh?–*Look at the piece again* – Kenny Swain, Dennis Mortimer, Gordan Cowans. What's that fella's name, blondie fella – Gary Shaw, that's it. How many's that? Ten – *Open the fuckin paper* – Who was the other bloke? Used to know all of these. Oh yeh, Peter Withe. How the fuck could I forget Peter Withe. What a goal, Peter. A goal to grace any final. Where have you gone, Peter Withe? Champions of Europe. Champions of Europe – *Open the fuckin paper, now.*

I turn to the piece on the boys and stare hard at the picture again, at the faces of the men on the roof. Fuck, I know every one of them.

I'm not grieving for them though. I'm grieving for me. I've been sharing needles with them all me life, in their gaffs, down the estate, in The Joy. I must have the virus too. Nothing fuckin surer. I'm going to die.

Maybe I've always known. It still comes as a shock, though. I'm going to die. I wonder which one of those cunts I caught it from – or which ones I gave it to. With me dirty blood.

Blame is a waste of time and energy, but. We're all to blame. And none of us is to blame. We never knew about the virus when we started on the gear. How the fuck were we to know you could get it from someone else's spike? But then we did know. They told us, the experts did. And we never gave a bollix anyway. Even after they took Carl out of his cell in The Joy and released him when they found out he had it, it never frightened us, you know. We never changed our ways. Fuck warnings, we said. There were always warnings about smack and what it does to you and we ignored all of those because ... because heroin is so bleedin good ... And the thing is, when you're all sitting round in a gaff and you're strung out, thinking that you're going to die, you grab the nearest works to you. You don't even ask who used it last, never mind ask them for a brief outline of their recent sexual and drug history. It's the same story in The Joy. If someone's had a turn-on and offers you whatever's left on the filter, you grab his spike and get it into you before he has a chance to change his mind. End of story.

End of story for me, anyhow.

I'm going to die.

Going ...

I don't know whether I should take the test. Perhaps it's better that I don't know. But I do know. I think. It's weird all that medical stuff. There's doctors who tell you that smoking is good for you and that eating oranges is a cure for bleedin cancer. Then other doctors will say that they're talking through their arses. There's loads of grey areas is all I'm saying. I've heard of blokes who rode birds with the virus and never caught it. There's people reckon you can get it from holding hands. Or French-kissing. Or sitting on the jacks. There's probably someone out there who reckons that sharing needles has fuck-all to do with it. You never know. I might be negative.

"You're positive," the doctor says. There's no preparing yourself for something like that. I feel like I'm having an out-of-body experience. It's like I'm not sitting here in the prison surgery at all. Everything looks black and white to me. Every sound is muffled. Everything is happening in slow motion. Numbed into silence. I can hear the doctor talking in a real sympathetic voice, but I'm not really listening to what he's saying. I pick out the odd word: " ... drugs ... safe sex ... not the end of the world ... go on living ... it's only a word, not a sentence. Remember that ..."

I manage to get me head together to ask him a question. "Doctor, what is HIV anyway?"

"We don't know a terrible lot about it yet, but what we do know is that it breaks down your immune system, so that a simple 'flu, for instance, could turn into pneumonia. And then–"

"I could die," I interrupt.

He nods at me, real solemn, like. He roots around in his desk and hands me some pamphlets, about different kinds of medication I can take and safe sex methods, though what good they are to me in here is beyond me. I feel a bit sorry for the bloke, having to break news like this to people all the time. Probably has to do it a few times a week and he doesn't look as though it gets any easier.

But during a sleepless night back in me cell, me tears are all for me. I'm going to die. I haven't been given a date, but every hour that passes is sixty minutes closer to the end. I decide not to tell me family about it. The shame of it is too much. For now, anyhow.

The next morning I decide to go to Mass. Turning to God in me hour of need. I'll talk to him. Pray. Pray that I'll get better. Stranger things have happened. Miracles, like. You read about it all the time. I'm sitting at the back of the church, when an old mate of mine from Dublin comes in. Mass is the only chance you ever get to talk to blokes from other wings when you're in prison, which explains why the church is such a popular place. Has fuck-all to do with God and all that shite. He sits on the bench beside me and we fall into this real sentimental chat about the old days and about home. He knows something's up with me. "What's the matter?" he says.

I don't know why, but I decide to tell him. "I've got the virus, man."

"Are ye sure?" he asks me.

I nod. "Doctor told me yesterday. I don't know what to fuckin do."

"Sure, I've got it as well," he says, dead cool, like, as though we're talking about satellite TV or something.

"Really?"

"Yeh. Sure, you can live for twenty years with it. Thirty even, so they say. You might never die from it. Someone without the virus might go out tomorrow and get hit by a fuckin bus. That's life, man."

"S'pose so."

"I'm right. I know what I'm talking about. The virus and the Aids are different things, man. The thing is, if you start to think about it and start to let it get you down, you'll give up the will to live and then you will die. Happened to a mate of mine in here. Had the virus for years he did and hadn't a clue about it. Then he found out and he started getting all depressed, you know. Just waiting for the day he was gonna die. He was too down to do an'thin. Stopped eating, lost loads of weight. His immune system was already fucked, but sure what with not eating and that he got this full Aids thing, you know. Died of a heart-attack, he did. I always told him that he'd have been better off never knowing."

"I think I'm the same as him."

"Nah. Thing to remember is, it's only a word, man, not a sentence." He must have been diagnosed by the same doctor as me. Everyone's reciting off the "Our Father" when he turns to me. "So are you going down the basement then?"

"The basement?"

"Yeh, man. Down the Aids wing. That's where I am. It's fuckin great. They give you phy, any drugs you want. And then they release you early."

"They do in their fuck," I say in disbelief.

"Honest. There's guys down there are only a year into five-year sentences and they're letting them go because they've got the virus. They don't want the cunts dying in prison. Pneumonia, overdoses, suicide. It's all bad publicity for them. So they shove them into the Aids wing and then, after a while, let them back on to the streets."

"There has to be a catch."

"There's not. I'm telling ye, if you went down there, you'd be out on the streets again in three or four weeks."

I've only served three months of me sentence and the thought of getting out after four is too much. Whether he's taking the piss or not, I'm going to check it out. I ask for permission to go and look around and the medical officer escorts me down.

Me first impression is that it's exactly like he said it was. I look in through the window on the door of the first ward and everyone seems to be happy in there, spaced out of it on drugs. It's tidy and warm and homely, with that disinfectant-clean feel you get in hospitals. And I can't believe what I'm seeing at the far end of the ward. There's three fucking birds sitting on a bed chatting away. Beautiful-looking birds as well, looking very fuckable in their satin nightdresses and pink, fluffy slippers. In the same ward as the blokes? Why didn't he tell me about this? He could have saved his breath going on about drugs and early release and warm beds and all that shite. Spending the last few months in jail has kind of curtailed me sexual adventures, you know. And I'm getting a hard-on thinking about the amount of riding that goes on in here once the nurses say "lights out". Women. This can't be true.

I turn around to the medical officer. "What are the birds doing in there?"

"The what, mate?" He peers in through the window and then laughs nervously. "Em, they're not women," he says.

"What are they?" I ask, like a fucking eejit.

"Well, they're men."

"Men?"

"Yeh, they're all transvestites."

I can feel me cheeks burning. The embarrassment.

"Most of them have had the operation," he says.

"What operation?"

"The sex change operation."

"You mean they had their balls cut off?"

He laughs. "Yeh, if you put it like that." I shuffle uneasily.

"So," he says, "are you thinking of moving down here then?"

"No, not at all," I tell him. "Sure, I don't even have the virus. I was just curious about it, that's all."

I return to me cell, deflated by the whole experience. Even though I'm going to have to learn to live with being a social pariah meself, I still couldn't live among all those queers down in the basement, early release or not. I'll just soldier on in silence here and, when I'm released, go back to Ireland to make a new start.

Irony of ironies, I've just received a letter from the Home Office's Immigration and Nationality Department informing me that the Secretary of State has taken a very serious view of me conviction. I don't even know who the cunt is, but fair play to him for following my case with such keen interest. It makes me feel kind of important. Anyhow, the letter ends:

On this occasion he has decided not to institute deportation proceedings against you. If, in the future, you come to our adverse notice, serious consideration will be taken to enforcing your departure.

All right, I know when I'm not wanted, you know. When I get out, I'm heading back to Dublin anyway to face the music over that job I'm s'posed to have done. Back to The Joy, I know. Probably for a year, maybe two. But there's nothing for me in London and I need to be around people ... people I love. Yeh, love. Anyway, thinking about those transvestites, who've had the snip, I can't avoid the feeling that this country is headed for big, big trouble.

♦   ♦   ♦

NOTHING I CAN'T HANDLE

I bang me head off the wall. Two joints was all it was. Two bleedin lousy joints. I bang me head off the wall again. Two joints and I end up in the pad for the night. Wasn't worth it, but fuck, man, it had to be done. If he'd been allowed to get away with what he was after doing, then I might as well get the word "doormat" tattooed across me chest, and let everyone in The Joy walk all over me. There's lads in here whose idea of a good time is to sit next to some soft bloke during rec and just keep poking their fingers in his face. If one person gets away with it, then it becomes a new craze. Hit the bloke a clatter back and, while you might get battered for it, you'll be respected for standing your ground. Sometimes you have to fight to be a man. Kenny Rogers said that. Doesn't matter whether you're a good goer or not. You've got to be a contender. I bang me head off the wall again.

It started yesterday. Jemser was after getting a bit of hash in and he owed me from the last time I shared with him. The problem was that he was on a different landing to me. But we found a willing courier in Clacker, whose cleaning duties gave him licence to roam around the place. He said he'd collect it for me. He came back an hour later, though, to tell me there were problems. "King Kong is on the landing," he said.

"So what?" I asked him. "Just bang on Jemser's door and he'll come out and give it to you."

"I did," he said. "He mustn't have heard me."

"Well, why didn't you give the door a boot?"

He just gave me this gormless look. He was probably just shiteing in case he got snared. But when you're put in such a position of responsibility, you owe it to your fellow prisoners to exploit it to the maximum and if that means ferrying drugs from wing to wing, then that's your duty.

The bell sounded for recreation then and, as we all walked down the stairs, I saw Jemser on the opposite landing and shouted over to him. "What's the story with that stuff?"

"I'll give it to Clacker to give to you after rec," he shouted back.

I waited in me cell all night and there was no sign of it, but. I was bulling when I got up this morning, but Jemser completely wrong-footed me when I confronted him over it in the library. "Did you get that bit of hash last night?" he said. Before I'd even had a chance of open me mouth.

"What bit of hash? I never got any hash."

"I sent yer man, Clacker, over with it. Enough for two joints there was. I would've given you more, but that's all I had to spare 'cos I had to fix up six other blokes."

"Hang on a sec," I said. "I didn't get any hash. Are ye sure you gave it to Clacker?"

"Yeh. He came for it around nine o'clock."

The bastard. I was just starting to think about various violent things I could do to the fucker to teach him a lesson, when I was called out for an unexpected visit. I went down to the visiting room. Table five, I was told, but I didn't recognise the bird who was sat on the other side. She was a ride, though. I double-checked it and it was the right table. I stalled for a bit, just staring at her, thinking the screws were taking the piss out of me. Then she said me name.

"Yeh," I said nervously.

"How are you?" she said, as though she'd known me for years, like. I still didn't have a bog who she was. Suddenly, she put her hands around me neck, pulled me halfway across the table and started wearing the face off me. Before I had the chance to respond in kind, I felt her tongue running over me teeth, trying to get in to me mouth. I opened up. Even with me eyes closed, I knew everyone in the room was looking at me. It was like I could feel the weight of their stares. I thought I was dreaming. Her lips were so soft, her tongue so moist, dancing around in me mouth. I felt me mickey stiffen up. Then all of a sudden it was over. And when she pulled her tongue out of me mouth, I could feel something inside. A small package. I rubbed it between me tongue and the roof of me mouth and it felt like a piece of clingfilm. Of course, I thought. A turn-on. It was the only reason why a beautiful bird I'd never met before would come into The Joy and stick her tongue in me mouth. Me boner eased as I slipped the package between the gum and me cheek.

"Who are you?" I asked.

"I'm Jackie, Gary's girlfriend."

Gary was a casual user who'd got out the previous day.

"There's twenty quid's worth there," she said.

"Tell him I said thanks."

We talked about Gary for a while. Now that he's out, she said, he was doing his best to keep off the gear and was going to try to straighten himself out. "Fucks up your life," I heard her say more than once. I'd said it more than once meself in me time.

As she talked, I started to think about the kiss and the gear in me mouth and laughing to meself at the thought of Gary not knowing he was after giving me two turn-ons in the one day.

When I got back up to me cell, I flicked on the radio and started cooking up. The powder dissolved quickly over the heat of me lighter and I drew up enough for one hit, leaving the rest on me spoon for later on. I sat on me piss-pot and examined me left arm, choosing a nice succulent vein. The steel pierced me skin and I let it go. It was amazing gear. I drew a deep breath in as I felt the rush and then I felt me head tip backwards and hit the wall. I exhaled slowly, enjoying every second of this full-body orgasm. Gary's chances of staying off the gear were pretty fuckin non-existent if this was the kind of stuff he could get.

I was still buzzing when I went to get me tea. Sleeping was going to be difficult unless I got a bit of hash to bring me down. I was just saying to meself how it was a pity I didn't have any when I saw Clacker coming down the stairs with his teapot and joining the queue. He'd robbed hash on me. I decided to kick the shit out of him. I just couldn't fight the urge. He'd probably spent the day telling people how he put one over on me and what a pushover I was.

"Next!" the screw on the urn shouted in my face, stirring me from my daydream. I collected me tea and made a point of passing Clacker in the queue. The shifty little fucker wouldn't even look me in the eye, a sure sign of guilt. Without taking me eyes off him, I climbed the stairs to the landing and walked backwards into the first cell to wait for him. "What's the story?" a voice behind me said. It was Bottler.

"Would you mind if I stood in here a second?" I said.

"Who are ye going to get?" he asked. He sounded excited, obviously hoping it was someone he didn't like.

"You'll see in a minute," I told him. Me only worry was the two screws chatting on the landing. "Do us a favour," I said to him. "Will you go over and distract them?"

"How?"

"Tell them you need a new toothbrush or a bar of soap or something from the stores."

As he sauntered down, I could see Clacker coming up the stairs with his pot of tea and I stood inside the door, clutching me own pot in me hand. I could hear his footsteps on the stairs and along the landing floor, getting louder as he approached. When he was just outside, I struck, throwing the pot full of scalding tea straight into his face. His reaction surprised me. There was no screaming. He just stood there, in a state of shock, blinking hard and shaking his head. I knew that before he got himself together again I had to finish the fucker off, so I took me empty teapot and smashed him across the face with it twice. His nose opened up and he staggered backwards, blood cascading down his face. Two of the lads managed to catch him before he fell back down the stairs.

I turned and legged it back to me cell, jumping on the bed and wiping the smatterings of blood off the side of the pot with me sleeve. Duffo, from three doors down, was into me like a light with his teapot in his hand. "Screws see you?" he asked.

"Dunno. I think one of them did."

"Here, have half of my tea," he said, pouring it into me jug. "That way, if they ask if it was you, you can just show them all the tea you've got left."

He went back to his cell and a screw duly arrived up. "Were you involved in that fight on the landing?" he said.

"What fight?" I said, real innocent.

"Did you throw tea over Clacker?"

"Wasn't me," I tell him, holding the jug towards him. "Sure, I've loads of tea left."

He nodded and left, allowing me to think I'd got away with it, until he reappeared with three other screws and I was ordered out. I was marched down the landing and thrown in here for the night. So here I am, just banging me head off the padded walls. Two joints. Was it worth it? Of course it was. I had to do him, the thieving bastard.

Doesn't matter whether it was two joints or two hundred. In here, you're only as good as your reputation. You're only as good as your last fight.

I'm thinking about Clacker. Wondering about his injuries. Last week, a couple of guys in the kitchen were talking about maybe scalding themselves to try and get a bit of compo out of the prison. They reckoned that scalding yourself with leaf tea left a permanent wine-coloured stain on you, whereas just boiling water or tea made with the bags didn't. The pot I threw over Clacker had leaf tea in it. I hope it's left a great big, plum-coloured birthmark the shape of Ireland on his face, so that every time he shaves he's reminded of the time he tried to fuck me over.

◆　◆　◆

JUST ANOTHER MOUNTJOY
HORROR STORY

There's puke all over me chin, on me cheeks and in me hair and its bitter, eggy smell is making me want to vomit even more, but still I haven't the will or the strength to lift me hand to wipe it off. There's a wet, slushy sensation in me jocks. I'm hoping against hope that it's sweat, but I know it's not. I get the auld trots really bad when I'm coming off the gear. I feel like shite, too low even to lift the covers and have a look at the state I've left the bed in.

Sweating. Sweating. Sweating.

Cold. Cold. Cold.

I want to pull the duvet up around me chin, but it's easier to lie here freezing than to move. I don't know if I can move. I don't want to know. Being still feels safer.

Cold. Cold. Cold.

The nightmares are about to begin, but I don't know whether I'm asleep or awake. I think I'm awake because it can't be possible to feel this kind of pain in your sleep. But I must be asleep, because these thoughts I'm having are coming from the darkest corners of me mind, the kind that only nightmares can access. Horrible, fuckin horrible thoughts. I'm bleedin psychotic. No, son. You don't have to be asleep to have nightmares. Let the show commence ...

Can I help you, sir?

Yes, ye bitch, you fuckin can.

How may I help you, sir?

For starters, you can hand me over all the money in the till or else I'll smash your fuckin face in.

I'm sorry, sir. We don't have such credit facilities in this store.

See this hammer? Do you need a fuckin closer look?

I'm sorry, sir. It's store policy. Perhaps you could try Kennedy's down the road.

Look, I'll kill you. I'll fuckin *kill* you, so I fuckin will. I'm desperate.

If sir is experiencing financial difficulties, perhaps he would like to choose his Christmas presents from our bargain department in the basement. There's ten percent off all items.

Bang! Bang! Bang!

NEEE-NAAW, NEEE-NAAWW, NEEE-NAAWW.

Tap. Tap. Tap. Order in the court, please. You stand before us here today charged with the crime of murder. How do you plead?

Murder.

It's an open-and-shut case, your honour. The accused is a junkie.

Junkie scum. Fucking junkie scum. Sell anything for smack. Sell the telly. Sell the cat. Sell the mother. Sell your hole.

I'm no faggot!

Well, we know your sort.

Guilty ... heinous crime of murder ... lack of remorse ... maliciously .... defenceless shop assistant ... prepared to hand over the money ... killed her anyway ... welfare reports ... life imprisonment ... Tap. Tap. Tap.

I can't get into me cell. There's too many people in there. A big audience for today's show. Queenie is trussed up like a turkey and hung upside down by his legs. The Hulk puts a rat into Queenie's mouth and then he tapes it up. There's only one way for the rat to go. Down his throat. Down, down, down. Into his stomach. He eats all of the undigested food in there. Then he tries to find his way out the other end. But Baldy has taped up his arse as well. Queenie is screaming. Only one way for the rat to go now. To eat his way through his stomach wall. The Hulk pulls out a stainless-steel cutlery set. "Wedding present," he says. Everyone laughs. Then he takes one of the knives and sticks it in Queenie's body. Round of applause. Then he sticks the rest of the knives in. Queenie bleeds. Stuck pig. "And for my next trick ..." Baldy sticks all the forks in his body. Oh! No-one can believe it. Then there's a drum roll. He's going to do it. He's going to stick the dessert spoons in him. Can we have silence, please? Can he do it? Yes!

"Quick!" Queenie shouts at me. "Get the screws before he pulls those teaspoons on me. Please. Help me."

I run out of the cell.

You grass. You fuckin rat.

'Scuse me. Flanno. Come quickly. Queenie is in trouble.

Queenie is like you, you cunt.

What do you mean?

Queer.

I'm not queer.

Oh yes, you are. I've seen your medical records. You've got the virus.

That doesn't mean nothing.

Means that you're a faggot.

Doesn't.

It's a faggot's disease.

Not any more, it's not. You can get it from birds. You can get it from needles.

Needles, me bollix. You've got Aids, you're a bender, end of story.

Most of the new cases coming on stream are actually heterosexual—

Face it. Face what you are.

Look, I've never been with a man in me life.

Well, then, how do you know you're not bent? How can you know unless you try it?

AIDS. Acquired Immune Deficiency Syndrome.

Freddie Mercury.

Rock Hudson.

Liberace.

Me.

No such thing as innocent victims. They got what they deserved. All of them. Who cares?

Q. How did Aids get into America?

A. Up the Hudson.

Q. What did the priest say at Freddie Mercury's funeral?

A. That's the cleanest hole he's ever been in.

Laughter. Cue applause. Clap, clap, clap.

The joke is on you. This time.

Sorry, sir. The switch is connected to an automatic timer. If you'd like to come back and threaten me with that hammer tomorrow, I'd be happy to oblige.

Automatic timer? What do you mean?

Panic button. 999.

Oh, no. Place is crawling with pigs.

Give yourself up. Drop your hammer and come out with your hands in the air.

You've grassed me, you bitch.

Twenty years. *Twenty* years.

Me eyes are open now and the nightmare has stopped. But the nightmare is only just beginning. Me body is still in convulsions, shuddering. Me arse especially is shaking, me loins going up and down like I'm riding an invisible woman. I've got a boner. It's the first in ages. The gear robbed me of the pleasure of having a good, hard erection, but there it is now, standing to attention. Standing proud.

Not for much longer, though. I've decided I can't go through with this any more. This was hell. But nothing compared to what comes next. Months and months of depression, hopelessness, desperation. No, a fuckin lifetime of it. That's what I can't face. Not in here anyhow. When I get out, that's the time to get meself sorted. In the morning, I'm gonna go down and see Duffo about getting a turn-on.

◆　　◆　　◆

UNFINISHED LETTERS

Dear Martina,

Do you remember me? Remember we went out together years ago? If you don't then I feel like such an arsehole, but if you do, please don't rip this up without reading it. I just need someone to talk to. I have something to say. Something that I've been wanting to tell someone for ages now. I'm not sure if you're going to laugh or cry or not care one way or the other. Then again, if you don't remember me, you're not going to care, are you? I remember you, Martina. I'll never be able to forget you. Anyway, the thing I wanted to say is difficult for me. It's just that something's wrong with me. I've got the virus. There. Said it. I've got the virus. I think from sharing needles. Now don't worry about anything. I'm not writing to tell you that you could have it as well. I only got this after we broke up, so don't be scared or anything, right?

I found out about it when I was inside in England. To be honest, it's kind of difficult to know how to feel. Physically I'm fine. And that's the most confusing thing. Being told you're going to die when you feel sick, it's easy to believe. But I feel fine. I won't always though. The doctors have told me I'm going to have to start looking after myself, because a cold could turn into pneumonia, what with my immune system in bits. But sure, where's the incentive to be looking after yourself if you know you're going to die anyway?

And then just when I'm starting to feel that way, some other expert messes with my head by saying that you can live for years with the virus and never get what they call full-blown Aids. I don't know. Makes no sense at all if you ask me. I just feel like I'm in a limbo waiting for the disease that's going to kill me to arrive. Sorry to depress you like this. I just had a few things I wanted to get off my chest and I also wanted to tell you not to worry about yourself, because I've only got this since we split up. I know that for a fact. So you don't have it ...

◆　　◆　　◆

Unhappy Christmas

Gary Glitter's "Another Rock and Roll Christmas" is playing in the waiting room. If there's one consolation about being locked up for the month of December, it's that at least you don't get to hear all those crap Christmas songs they play endlessly in the shops when you're trying to get a bit of auld shopping together. Today is Christmas Eve and, by the time the screws let me out in half an hour or so, I'll have missed the worst parts of it, the Cliff and Shakey Christmas retros, the ads for toys that look fuck-all like they did on the telly once you take them out of their boxes and the panic buying of food and presents that will never be used.

Kept me nose clean these last few months, I have. So they're letting me out, just for the Christmas. The second they open that gate, I'm heading into town, either to buy a few presents meself or to get a few pints into me. It's a straight choice between last minute shopping or me first decent drink in ages. It's odds on the pub will win. I'm due a drink at this stage anyway. The last couple of months in here have been a real downer, what with Derek topping himself and that.

Derek was sound. We were never what you'd call good mates, but we were as friendly as two junkies can be in each other's company. If he saw you in the street or the pub, like, he'd pull you over and tell you he was on the lookout for chequebooks. He'd give you a tenner for any you could get your hands on. A tenner sounds fuck-all, I know, but if you'd just snatched some auld one's bag and were going through the horrors, then Derek was your shortcut to getting some gear into you. He didn't use so much himself these days. He was knocking on a bit and he considered it a miracle of medical science that he'd managed to use for so long without getting the virus or any organ problems or nothin. He didn't want to push his luck, ye know.

Anyhow, Derek thought he'd be sitting here with us today, waiting to get out for the Christmas to see his family and that. He only had a few months left to serve so he put in for early release, built up his hopes and then got knocked back. I don't know who came to visit him that afternoon, but he was really cut up when he went back to his cell, knowing he was going to have to serve out the last few months while everyone else was outside enjoying themselves. He had got a bit of hash in, and he lay on his bed and smoked himself deeper and deeper into depression. Then he wound a sheet around his neck and hanged himself.

It was heavy shit. The guy had fuck-all time to serve. Such a waste of fuckin life, man. Anyway, no-one really felt the same about Christmas after that and I'm glad to be escaping the atmosphere in here.

We knew Derek was feeling shite. But nobody said nothin. You can't show affection or concern towards another man in here without being called a queer or a steamer. You don't think that other prisoner's hurt and pine and worry and cry as much as you do when they're in their cells alone at night. To people on the outside, we don't matter in here. Everyone thinks we're vermin and the sad truth is we believe it now ourselves.

Derek made it on to the radio. The headlines, something he was never able to do when he was alive. Twenty-five years on the earth and the only newsworthy thing he did was to take his own life. The bird on the radio reads out the report, giving sketchy details about him and how he killed himself. There's no explanation why. The public will never know. Or give a fuck. The fact that he stuck his head in a noose and strangled himself or slashed his wrists or whatever will satisfy their sense of curiosity. They don't want to know what kind of person he was, what kind of mate, what kind of son, what kind of brother. Or what made him do it.

I've decided not to go for a pint now. I'm going home. Home to see me ma and da. I have no gifts to bring them, but I think they'll understand. I just want to wish them a Merry Christmas and tell them that I love them.

◆　◆　◆

A FRIEND IN NEED

"Look, what's the fucking story? Are yiz getting out or what? I've a bleedin living to make. Stop fluting around and tell me where yiz are wanting to go."

Shut the fuck up, I said in me mind. I needed a bit of quiet to get me head round this.

Taxi drivers were never me favourite people, but this one was a particularly cranky bastard even by their standards. He was in a snot just because he had the misfortune of picking up three junkies out trying to score. I was sure he'd have preferred some respectable, four-eyed, middle-class suit he could bore the ears off, going on about tax and crime and the Government and the roads and the price of a pint, prefixing every little criticism with the words, "They can send a man to the moon and they can't even ..."

I was tempted to tell him that, despite the fact that they can send a man to the moon, it's still nearly impossible to score smack in Dublin this afternoon, but he didn't need telling. He'd had the full guided tour of Dublin's junk spots in the previous forty minutes. Fuck-all outside the drug clinic on Pearse Street. Fuck-all on Wexford Street. Fuck-all in York Street flats. Fuck-all off Harcourt Street. Fuck-all down the Bond. Even the fella who usually stood at the corner of

Meath Street there, selling gear openly like it was apples and oranges, was having a day off.

There was already twenty notes on the meter, but still the driver was moaning about all the driving around and waiting he was having to do. Sure, they don't want to work these days. He looked at me like I was a pubic hair that he'd just pulled out of his ham sandwich. "Tell me where youse are wanting to go or fuck off out of me cab," he said.

What the fuck. "Ballymun," I told him.

"Are you sure?"

"Yeh."

"Right, well you'd better be, because I'm dropping you there."

For town-heads like us, going to the Mun was always a last resort. You had to accept that there was at least an evens chance you were going to have your gear robbed on you and your head kicked in. Quite often, a dealer who sold you gear would have a few blokes waiting for you downstairs to mug you on your way out. There's dealers in the Mun who have sold the same bag of smack ten times in the one day. We had to take a chance though. Dekker, sitting in the back, said nothing. He was too strung out to voice an opinion. All he knew was that he needed gear inside him, but he didn't have the energy to argue with anyone about it. Me mate Mick was in the horrors too. And I was starting to suffer as well. Me shirt was sapping under me jacket and me skin was starting to feel all tender. I was shivering like fuck. I thought we'd never get there and I think the driver was getting off on driving as slowly as he could.

He eventually dropped us at the flats and I paid him. Dekker somehow found the energy to get out of the car. It was like he smelled the gear, the remedy for his fuckin misery. Dicey's flat was way up the top of the block and, surprise su-fucking-prise, the lift was broke. It must have taken about ten minutes to drag our bodies up the stairs, holding on to the banisters all the way, but once we discovered that

Dicey was in and open for business, we all started to feel a lot better. Me and Dekker scored a couple of turn-ons each and Mick, the jammy cunt, had enough for five.

We were paranoid as fuck leaving the gaff, but there was no-one waiting for us at the end of the stairwell. We were excited then, thinking that we were out of the woods. Stupid, of course. In the distance, I could see a gang of Mun heads standing under the archway, all looking in our direction. "Is there another way out of this place?" I asked.

"Why, what's the story?" said Dekker.

"The welcoming committee," I said, nodding me head towards the gang.

"You're not scared of them, are ye?" Mick said, laughing.

"I'm not scared," I said. "It's just they'll know we're fucking town-heads, right? They'll know we're up here for gear and they'll take the stuff off of us."

Mick looked at me. "Well, there isn't any other way out. If they want it, we'll just have to give it them."

We carried on walking towards them, trying not to look like the shiteing cunts we were. Our body language was giving us away, though. But as we got to the archway, I recognised one of the lads. It was Jazzer, an auld mate of mine from inside. He was one of the few spot-on blokes in The Joy. We used to share everything: burn, smack, papers. He was the one who taught me how to make me own syringes. And we were a formidable doubles-team at the auld pool, clearing a table in the time it takes to rack one up. Or very near it.

When he called out me name, the other boys couldn't believe their luck. "You know yer man?" Dekker asked.

"Yeh, I do," I said, all smug, like. "Listen, we're sorted, lads. We're old mates from inside."

"How's it going, my man?" Jazzer shouted as he came over to me. He grabbed the top of me arm in a gesture which I took to mean that he was pleased to see me but didn't want to hug me in front of his mates.

"Sound as a pound, man," I said. "What're you up to?"

"Ah, this and that, you know. I'm still on the gear, like."

"Still?" I said. "When we were in The Joy, ye said you were gonna get off it, once you got out, like."

"Yeh, I did say that, didn't I? I did for a while. Ah, you know what it's like yourself."

I nodded. I knew only too well.

"So, you still on it?" he asked.

"The odd time," I said. I'm a liar.

"So, what brings you up here? Were yiz scoring?"

"No, not at all. Just calling up for a mate of ours. He's not in." I tried to change the subject then. "So, do you remember me and you on the auld pool table inside, do you?"

"Ah, now you're bringing me back." He looked at his mates. "See this cunt here?" he said, pointing at me. "A fucking shark, man. A fucking shark on the pool table. Best doubles team in The Joy, we were."

Dekker and Mick looked as though they were getting a bit tired of our reminiscing and like they needed a turn-on rapid, so I told Jazzer we must get together for a gargle sometime and went to walk off.

"Where do yiz think yiz're going?" he said, blocking me way.

"What?"

"Gimme your gear."

I looked at him. "Are you joking, are you?"

He turned his head and looked at his mates and then back at me. "Gimme your fuckin gear or we'll kick the fuck out of you."

"I've only got one turn-on," I said, as the rest of the Mun heads surrounded us.

"Well, fuckin hand it over."

141

I stuck me hand in the pocket of me jeans, pulled out one of me packages and handed it to him.

Dekker did the same. Mick, the cunt who had the nerve to call me scared, handed over all five of his to the scrawny little bollix who was going through his pockets. Jazzer put all the gear in his pocket and went off.

It started to piss rain. Bang on time too, because the weather kind of reflected our own mood as we walked off out of the flats, none of us knowing what to say to each other. We couldn't even afford a taxi to get back to town. I was freezing. The pain that was screaming in me stomach told me I needed to get this turn-on into me fast. Me skin felt like millions of little ants were swarming all over it. The drenching we were getting didn't help. We were all feeling really sorry for ourselves.

"I've a good mind to ring the pigs," Dekker said eventually. Typical of him to try and look on the bright side, but we weren't in the mood for jokes. Especially Mick. At least me and Dekker had a turn-on left. We had the means to help us forget about this whole shite trip, for a few hours at least.

Halfway up the road, Mick stopped. "Let's go back," he said.

"No, just leave it," me and Dekker said together.

But he persisted. "Fuck them. We're not gonna let them get away with it, are we? A few Mun heads."

The angry way he said "a few Mun heads" got me and Dekker fuming as well. We started to think seriously about it. "We don't know where they are, though," Dekker said.

"We do," Mick said, pointing. "They went that way."

Mick didn't seem as sick as he was in the taxi on the way out. It was anger overcoming his sickness. That happens you sometimes. We all turned round and headed back towards the flats, Mick striding off in front and me and Dekker following, unable to keep up. We couldn't believe our luck. Standing on a corner, all on his lonesome, like, was the scrawny little cunt who went through Mick's pockets. He looked like he was dealing the gear he was after robbing off us. There was no sign of Jazzer and the rest of the boys. Dekker called the fucker and, not recognising us from before, he came over. "What are youse looking for, lads?" he asked us. "Smack, is it?"

Mick grabbed him by the scruff of his neck. "Give us our gear back, ye little prick."

You could see the realisation register on the bloke's face. "Eh, I haven't got it."

"Give us our fucking gear," Mick said again, screwing up his face, real evil, like.

"I've already told you. I don't fuckin have it."

I didn't see Mick go to his pocket, but suddenly he had a long steel drill bit in his hand. He held it in his fist like a dagger, drew his arm right back and then smashed the fella right in the face with it. The noise of the cunt's cheek opening up was like the sound of a piece of cloth being ripped. It was a serious wound. Yer man collapsed into a puddle of rainwater and the blood was pumping out of him onto the path. I bent down and went through his pockets. He only had four of the turn-ons on him. We didn't hang around to ask him about the other three. He was losing blood and consciousness fast.

REHABILITATION

S.W.A.L.K.

There's another new culchie after moving on to our landing and he's getting deaths off the lads. This morning, on the way down to slopping out, six of them emptied their piss-pots under his door. Maybe I'm getting cynical about all this them-and-us shite that goes on between the Dubs and culchies in here and seeing it for what it is. If there were only Dubs in this place, then it would be northsiders against southsiders. If there were only northsiders, it'd be Summerhill against Ballymun. If a load of English blokes were put in here tomorrow, we'd all gang together and pour piss under their doors and attack them with toothbrush blades. It's all tribal bollix. None of it matters a fuck, because none of us matters a fuck. End of story. So what's the point in fighting?

Fighting isn't my thing. Well, not today anyhow. I'm after getting a letter from the lads down the estate. Dead nice of them to keep in touch, even though I never read the fuckin things meself. In fact, the censors in here could probably tell you how Duffo and Redser are getting on better than I could. Being a censor in The Joy must be a screw's nightmare. A lot of the lads in here would be either barely able to write or dyslexic. Even those who can write, often go on for pages and pages about all the dirty things they'd like to do to their birds if they were with them.

Anyway, this letter hasn't come through the censors. I had it sneaked in. It's not really the letter I'm after. It's the envelope. I've heard stories before about the prisoners in here, years and years ago, getting in letters with the stamps soaked in LSD. The prison copped on to it, though, and now they tear them off the envelopes along with the flaps before they give them to us. Time has moved on. Drugs have moved on as well. Who fuckin takes LSD in here any more? Fuckin no-one. Ecstasy, man. That's the latest. And along with new drugs come great new ways to smuggle them in. The boys have broken the E into small pieces, licked the glue on the envelope flap, put the tiny bits down on to it and then sealed the envelope. This tablet seems to have been broken up much smaller, though. The lads have done a good job this time. I lick me finger and start to rub at it. A corner of the flap turns up and I start to pick at it and tease it off slowly. Gently. I peel it off altogether. You can see the white fragments and the powder clearly on the gluey bit. I crumple the flap up into a ball and put it into me mouth, chewing up the paper. Any minute now, I'm going to be jumping up the fuckin walls. I lie back on me bed, waiting for the E to kick in. The paper starts to dissolve in me mouth.

Okay, here goes, hold on tight now ...

◆　◆　◆

OH IRELAND, WE LOVE YOU!

Townsend is stood over the ball on the edge of the box and the Romanians have lined up a wall. The man to watch, though, is Sheedy, who can fuckin fair hit them from this kind of range. The ref blows the whistle. Townsend taps the ball back to Sheeds, who chips it up onto his own foot and hits it over the top and straight at the keeper. Our heads are in our hands. What a waste. Fannying around with free-kicks like he's Zico and fucking Socrates. No need to panic, though. It's still only the first half. A quick look round for the screws and I take another long slug out of me cup and a blast off me joint and join the chorus:

147

Come ... on ... you ... boyz in gree-en,
Come on you boyz in gree-en,
Come on you boyz,
Come on you boyz in gree-en ....

Houghton's having a stormer. His cross finds Sheeds, who swings it back across the box. McGrath chases. He goes down. "Penalty!" we all shout together, though few of us actually saw what happened and, even when the action replay refutes our argument, we still turn to one another and nod, "Definite penalty."

Raymo, who's sitting up the front with the rest of the square eyes, leads us into a chant of "the referee's a wanker".

It said in the *Star* this morning that Ireland was going to grind to a standstill for this game. An air of expectation hangs over the country, it said. Here in the middle row, the only thing that's hanging everywhere is the whiff of the hooch we're knocking back and the sickly sweet stink of hash which we're smoking as much to take the taste of the hooch out of our mouths as to get stoned.

We're into the second half and Raymo continues to drown out George Hamilton's voice with a far more entertaining commentary of his own, the anxiety in his voice growing the longer we wait for the first goal. Another minute, another miss. "Youse couldn't score in a brothel with a fistful of fivers," Raymo screams.

We all roar laughing, though I'm not sure whether it's genuine laughter, nervous laughter or just giddiness from the hash. I light up another joint. Behind me, I notice that the boys are taking the piss out of Dumbo. They're after giving him a roll-up and telling him it's a joint and the fuckin eejit thinks he's getting high on it. "Wow," he says, taking in a deep breath and letting it go, "that's good gear, man."

"Here, eat this," someone says to him, handing him an orange.

"It'll help bring you down again."

He peels off a segment and no sooner has he popped the thing into his mouth, than he's telling us that the buzz is going away. I'm in knots laughing.

We're all part of Jackie's arm-mee,
We're all off to Ital-eeee,
And we'll really shake 'em up
When we win the Wor-uld Cup,
'Cos Ireland are the greatest football tee-um.

Fuck. The Romanian backlash we've been expecting materialises. Bonner does well to take the sting out of a long-range effort from that Raducioiu bloke. "They beat us," someone says, "and we're not fucking taking any more of their orphans, right?" Everyone laughs.

The lads are still winding up Dumbo. Not that I pity the thick cunt. He seems to be grateful for the attention he's getting anyway. He's doing life for knifing an auld one and no-one ever talks to him. All hostilities are suspended today, though. There's a ceasefire on for the match. It's not every day Ireland plays for a place in the quarter finals of the World Cup, ye know. Even the lads who are despised in here are being given blow. Even the knackers are sitting among blokes who wouldn't usually piss on them if they were on fire, discussing tactics and cracking jokes and everything.

Fuck, I don't even hate culchies today. Even the Cork lads who lashed me out of it last time I was shanghaied down there. They're sound enough fellas, just proud of their part of the country. The Lee, Larry Tompkins, multi-channel. They're sound. We're all on the same side. Dubs, culchies, murderers, queers, screws, psychos, grasses, rapists. We're all Irishmen. United Irishmen. North men, South men, comrades all, Dublin, Belfast ...

Raymo screams as Hagi goes on another run forward. He lets fly.

It's a fucking rasper. But Bonner manages to save it. A fucking hero, man. Me nerves are in tatters. I need another joint.

The final whistle is met by a huge sigh of relief. We survived the late Romanian onslaught. Extra time, it is.

Two, three, four ...
We are green, we are white,
We are fuckin dynamite,
Na-na-na-na,
Na-na-na,
Na-nah.

The most anxious-looking people in here are the screws, but. We should be back up in our cells now, but they know if they try to move us before this is over, we'll be up on the fuckin roof before you can say "extra time". Nobody says nothing to us about turning in, so we just take it that we're allowed stay up till the end and there's a rush for the jacks. I've been bursting for a shite since the start of the second half, what with the effect that hooch stuff has on your digestive system, I didn't really trust me arse. But I can't hold it for the whole of extra time.

For some reason, as I sit on the bowl I start thinking about that film, *Escape to Victory*. Sylvester Stallone, Pele, Michael Caine, Bobby Moore and Ossie Ardiles were all banged up in this German prisoner of war camp during the Second World War. For a bit of a propaganda exercise the Nazis decided to challenge them to a game of ball. The lads, seeing it as an opportunity to escape, agreed. So, match day arrived and, by half-time, the Allies were being slaughtered, four fucking nil or something. And they were playing brutal. Didn't matter, though, because come half-time they were all gonna hop into the tunnel that someone was after digging underneath the bath in their dressing-room and do a legger. Half-time came, the tunnel was finished and they were just about to leave, when Sylvester Stallone, I think it was, said he wanted to go back and finish off the match. "Hey, we can win this," he told the boys as they were all making their way to freedom. "Let's go out there and beat them." Fuck freedom, he said. The Germans are bating the shite out of us in the War, we can't let them beat us at ball as well. Ardiles said he'd go back and play. Pele was game as well. Bobby Moore said he was on for it and Michael Caine was persuaded as well. And they went back on to the pitch.

Stupid cunts. Or were they? As I flush the jacks, I realise why I'm thinking about that film. If the screws told us now that they were going to open the gates for fifteen minutes for anyone who wanted to escape, no-one would budge. There's a little bit of Sylvester Stallone in all of us tonight. We could be just half an hour away from being among the last eight teams in the World Cup. We can win this match, we're thinking. Let's go out there and beat them.

> *You'll never beat de Oy-rish,*
> *You'll never beat de Oy-rish.*

I go back to me seat and nobody's robbed the joint I left on it. Wonders will never fucking cease. Best supporters in the world. Best supporters in the fuckin world. Thank fuck the screws didn't see it.

The Romanians start on the attack again and Bonner gets down low to tip a shot wide. I look over me shoulder at the back of the hall, just to check the screws aren't watchin, and take a slug out of me cup of hooch. It's murder. I'm buzzing like a good thing here, but me mouth feels like I've been French-kissing a fuckin ashtray all night. I light up another joint as Ireland come forward. Quinn makes a run into the box. "Faster, faster, faster!" Raymo's shouting. "Jaysus, you'd run faster than that if Sneaky was after ye." Those of us who've been nicked by Sneaky can't help but laugh. A penalty shoot-out seems inevitable now. Then Sheeds makes a beautiful run into the box and nods the ball back to Houghton, who tries to lob the keeper with a header like he did Peter Shilton a couple of years ago in Germany, but this time it's just over the top. It's the best chance we get in extra time.

The ref blows up. We're all as shattered as the players, who fall down in the centre circle, have their cramps attended to and decide among themselves who's going to take the pennos. Big Jack looks as though he doesn't give a bollix. Coolest man in the stadium, he is. Fair play to him, I say.

> *Give it a lash, Jack,*
> *Give it a lash, Jack,*
> *Never, never, never say no,*
> *Ireland, Ireland, Republic of Ireland,*
> *Rev it up and here we go.*

Shite. The omens aren't good. The Romanians are going first, which kind of puts the pressure on us to keep scoring. Up comes Hagi, the fucker. The new Maradona, they're calling him, though if you ask me he's played more like fuckin Madonna today. He makes no mistake from the spot, but, and Raymo leads the chorus of boos. There's a hushed silence as Sheeds steps forward then. "Go on, Sheeds, ye boy ye," we shout. He's not scared to take the auld pennos, fair fucks to him. He blasts it straight, as the goalie dives. "Yes!"

Lupu, the flash bastard, walks up real nonchalant, places the ball and beats Bonner easily. I look back to make sure the screws aren't looking and take another long slug out of me hooch. Houghton's up next. Houghton, the little fuckin terrier. He won't let us down. He didn't in Stuttgart. He buries the thing and sinks to his knees. We raise our fists in triumph.

Rotariu bangs in Romania's third. Bonner guesses right, though, and I have the feeling that he's due to save one. Our nerves are fraying at the edges. The lads are even snapping at Raymo, who's kept us entertained all night. "Shut the fuck up," they're telling him. Here comes Townsend. What a player. Cool as a fish's fart. The little run-up and – "Yes!" – sends the keeper the wrong way.

The next Romanian to take a penno is Lupescu. I reckon he's had one already, but I'm told that I'm confusing him with Lupu. But the two cunts look like each other and I'm not entirely convinced. His penalty is Romania's worst so far, Bonner getting a firm hand to it but not firm enough to turn it round the post. Bollix. They've turned the screw again. Cascarino makes the lonely walk from the centre circle next. We all groan as he drills the bleedin thing low and it just about sneaks under the keeper's body. Blessed.

"Timofte?" someone asks as the Romanian's fifth penalty taker steps up. "That's fucking shampoo, isn't it?" It's funny. We're too much on edge to laugh, though. Some of the lads are even too much on edge to watch. This fella doesn't take any kind of run-up. He just stands over the ball and hits it, low to Bonner's right. Bonner's down like shot, he puts both his hands behind the ball and pushes it out. Pandemonium breaks out. We're screaming. We're standing on chairs. Score the next one and we're there. Who's taking it, we wonder. Then forward walks David O'Leary.

"What?" Raymo says in disbelief. "David O'Leary? Ah, for fuck's sake. Sure, he doesn't take pennos."

"He's never scored a goal for Ireland," George Hamilton reminds us.

"Me bollix," says Raymo. "Call him back, Jack. Don't let him take it. Please, Jack. What about Aldridge? Let him take it."

"He can't take one," I shout up to him, "'cos he's after being substituted."

"Well, let McCarthy or Moran or Quinn or someone take it. Or Bonner. He's allowed take one."

He's told to shut up. "That's it, we're out," he says, putting his hands over his eyes.

We all share his doubts. But O'Leary proves us wrong. He runs up and hits the ball to the right, far beyond the keeper's feeble effort to reach it. We go absolutely ape-shit, screaming, hugging each other, throwing hooch in the air like it was champagne. Through all the noise, Raymo's voice can still be heard: "I knew he wouldn't let us down. David O'Leary. What a player. Never doubted him. I told youse, didn't I?"

As we all file out to collect our tea, the lot of us are singing in a single voice:

One David O'Leary,
There's only one David O'Leary,
One David O'Leeeer-eeee ...

I don't ever want to see another drop of hooch in me life. Me breath's rancid and me tongue's cemented to the roof of me fuckin mouth. Even the tea can't take the taste away. I don't care, though, Jack's boys did the business. Give it a lash is right. I eventually nod off, with a familiar tune ringing around in me head:

Come ... on ... you ... boyz in gree-en,
Come on you boyz in gree-en
Come on you boyz ...

♦   ♦   ♦

A FORK IS OUT OF THE QUESTION

They call him Bottler. He thinks he's a hard case. I'm not afraid of him, but. And just because he's the best snooker player in this gaff, he thinks he can hog the table for the whole bleedin night.

He's really making a meal of this game, insisting on clearing all the colours, even though his opponent needs about twelve snookers to beat him and would probably readily chuck in the frame if Bottler wasn't too busy doing his Hurricane Higgins act to listen. He hardly has to move his bridge to put the yellow, green and brown away, blue slips easily into the middle pocket, he has a straight angle on the pink and then he pockets the black off three cushions, the flashy prick. He starts to rack up the reds again immediately for another game.

"Fancy a go?" I ask Redser.

He shakes his head. "We'll never get him off the table."

"Yes, we will. I'll tell him to fuck off it."

This English guy who I just know to see comes up and asks whether we fancy teaming up for a game of doubles with him and Grendox. There is only enough time left for one frame anyway, so a doubles match makes sense. That way everyone gets a game. We walk up to the table, where Bottler is chalking his cue, waiting for his next challenger. "What's the story," he says, "which one of youse wants to play me?"

"None of us," I tell him, "the four of us are having a game of doubles."

He laughs in me face. "Ask me bleedin bollix. We agreed we were playing winner keeps table at the start of rec. I haven't been beaten yet and I'm not leaving the table until I am."

I'm really pissed off now. "Fuck off, will ye. You're after having the bleeding thing for an hour and ten minutes. We always play doubles at the end, so everyone who's wanting a game gets one."

"What's it worth?" he says, sneering like.

"How do you mean?"

"Have you any cigarettes on you?"

"Cigarettes?"

"Yeh, cigarettes. If you give me a few auldsmokes, you can have it."

"I wouldn't give you the steam off me piss. You don't own the table, you know. So get out of the way."

He looks at me and then at Redser, Grendox and the English fella. He knows he's out-numbered, but, while he doesn't want his head kicked in, he doesn't want to lose face either. He asks me to follow him on up to his cell to sort it out, man to man, like. He goes on up the stairs and all the boys are asking me what I'm going to do.

"I'm gonna fight the cunt," I tell them, as if I have a choice. I take off me new leather, not wanting to get it torn, and go up after him. Me heart is going like a fuckin moped as I walk along the landing towards his cell. His door is wide open, but he doesn't seem to be in there. I call his name and there's no answer.

I look up and down the landing a couple of times and decide to go in and wait for him. Once I'm inside, I notice a shadow on the wall and realise that he's behind me, with his hand held high in the air and he's lunging towards me. I spin around and dive onto his bed and he misses me by just a few inches. He backs up a few steps, laughing like a maniac. He has a stainless-steel fork in his hand, with the four prongs bent inwards and melted together into one point, for stabbing with. "Come on, ye cunt," he says, gripping it hard in his fist.

"You scumbag," I say. "What about a straight go? With no weapons, like."

He laughs again. "What's wrong? Are you chicken?"

"Can you fight without weapons," I ask him, "or are you the windy bastard everyone says you are?"

He gets really upset about that. "I'll show you who's a windy bastard," he says, charging towards me.

I grab his teapot off the table and smash him across the face with it. It stops him dead in his tracks and he drops the fork. He turns around. There's a gang of people out on the landing, some of them hoping to see him get a bating and some of them hoping to see me get one. Most are there to see both of us get one if the truth be told. Whether it is out of fear of me or of getting lagged by the screws, Bottler backs out of the cell and runs down the stairs.

This fucking rage comes over me. The bastard tried to stab me with a fork when I wasn't looking. I'm not going to disappoint this crowd. I decide to smash up his cell. I pull his radio off his table and smash it off the wall. I pull out his bedside locker and put me foot through the hardboard backing on it. I turn his chair upside down and break off one of the aluminium legs and use it to smash up anything he has of value. I tear his pictures and posters off the wall. Family photographs are shredded to pieces. His piss-pot looks like it hasn't been emptied for about three days. I kick it over and all this piss and shit is sent spilling across the floor. I tip over a basin of water he was steeping his socks in. His bed, one of those old steel hospital jobs, is too heavy for me to lift, so I just turn it over, making sure the mattress falls to the floor and soaks up his piss.

As I calm down and look at the mess I've made of his room, one of the lads tells me that a screw is on his way up. I slip out the door before he arrives. As I return to me cell, he's asking all the lads who wrecked Bottler's cell. But nobody saw anything.

◆　◆　◆

SOMETHING'S COOKING IN THE KITCHEN

It was a good deal. I knew I was on to a good thing. Carry all the tea churns from the kitchen to the dining room in return for an ounce of burn. "I'm your man," I told one of the screws in the kitchen. An ounce of burn was an ounce of burn and there were few other employment opportunities open to me. People think you spend your whole time in prison sewing mailsacks and baking bread. You don't. There's fuck-all work in here. Fuck-all work inside and fuck-all work outside. Story of me fuckin life. Couple of weeks ago, I was handed about five big bags of leather gloves, was put sitting at a table and was told to turn them all inside out. Duffo, who was sitting next to me, had to turn them all the right way round again and put them back into the bags. What a fucking waste of time. It did me bleedin head in, it did.

So I liked me new kitchen duties. Well, I did for about the first five weeks, until one particular Thursday afternoon. Slasher was in the kitchen as usual, chopping the vegetables. Still there, despite all the bragging he'd been doing about his plan to get out of The Joy within a week and with a few grand to help him to adjust to life on the outside. It involved a turnip, a cleaver, a slight slip of the hand, a severed finger, a lot of screaming, threats of litigation, an out-of-court cash settlement and an early release. But try as he did, he just couldn't take that cleaver to his finger.

I always felt sorry for Slasher. He never really settled down to life inside, which is fair enough. The pigs had lifted him at his da's funeral, frogmarched him straight to the cop shop. No sooner was his auld fella in the ground, than Slasher was in the police station answering questions about some bank robbery in town, which he eventually went down for. But he was always going on about getting out again.

One of the other lads must have read me mind this day. "Here, I thought you were gonna cut your finger off," he said to him. Accusingly, like.

"I am," Slasher said, without lifting his eyes from the turnips.

"When?"

He didn't answer. Everyone started calling him a shiter then, and chicken-shit and all.

"Look," he said after a while, "it's easier said than done."

"Well, why do ye keep bleedin goin on about it then?" he was asked.

"You were the one who fuckin brought it up."

"Only 'cos you've been saying you're gonna do it for ages. Except you're too much of a fuckin woman to do it."

It was obvious that the lads weren't going to leave him alone. They wanted blood. They were all singing, "Shiter! Shiter! Shiter!" like a bunch of kids ganging on a young fella in a playground.

Slasher just folded. "All right, I'll do it," he said, putting down a turnip and picking up the cleaver. An audience gathered round. He slapped his hand down on the worktop and closed his fist, leaving just his little finger sticking out. He held the chopper tight in his hand and pulled it back. He was trembling.

"Go on, do it!" we were shouting at him. "Hurry the fuck up before the screw comes back."

It was a straight choice between losing a finger and losing face. But he just couldn't do it. He was probably asking himself the same questions we were, whether much blood would be spilt, whether it was possible to cut the bone clean in half with the cleaver or whether he'd botch the job and leave the top of his little finger flapping about, still attached to his hand by a small piece of flesh.

"I'll do it for ye," we heard a voice say. It was Jacko, one of the lads off the landing. None of us thought the bloke was serious.

"I'll do it for ye, right?" he said again.

Slasher looked a bit surprised too, but he just nodded and handed Jacko the cleaver.

"Now, are you sure you're wanting this done?" Jacko asked him, clamping Slasher's wrist on the worktop with his hand to make sure it didn't move.

"Yeh, go on," Slasher said. His voice was trembling.

Without flinching, Jacko threw his arm back and, real quick, brought the cleaver down hard on to the finger. And it just, like, fell off. Couldn't believe it, we couldn't. It was just sitting there. There was no blood, no bits of flesh or gristle or an'thin. Slasher was in too much of a state of shock to scream. He just stood there with his mouth open, white as a fuckin sheet. We were all in too much of a state of shock to say anything. Jacko was the first to talk.

"Here, look at that," he said, pointing at the finger. "Someone's after leaving a chip there."

He started breaking his bollix laughing, then calmly put the cleaver back on the table and sat down. Slasher, though, recovering from the first shock, started to scream real loud. One of the screws came charging into the kitchen: "What? What? What?"

"He's after cutting his finger off," I said, offering meself as an alibi.

"Yeh, we saw everything," said Jacko. "Chopping the few spuds, so he was, and whack, off it came. Clean as a whistle. Chop, chop, chop, chop, *bang*."

The screw looked at Jacko and then at Slasher, who was fuckin panic-stricken. "You cut your finger off?" he asked. "Look, tie it off and I'll call the medical officer."

One of the boys tore a strip from a tea-towel and wrapped it around his finger, while the screw picked up the phone and dialled the medical centre. "How're ye doin, sir?" he said. "Ah, can't complain meself. Listen, we've had a bit of an accident down here. Can you send someone round?"

Slasher let a roar out of him. "Hurry the fuck up, I'm losing blood here!"

By this stage, Jacko was grinning, sitting back with his feet on the table, his arms folded on his chest in front of him and his eyes never leaving Slasher. "He's gonna collapse," he said to me. "Look at the face on him. White as a fuckin ghost, he is. Definitely gonna faint."

"No, he's not," said one of the other lads.

"Betcha any money he passes out within the next sixty seconds."

"Tenner?"

"Right."

While the blood seemed to be draining from his face and his body getting weaker and weaker, Slasher somehow summoned up the energy to let out another scream. "Get me a fuckin doctor, ye bollix!"

Soon, the medics came and carted Slasher off to hospital. But he never got his early release in the end. There were rumours he got a bit of dosh out of the prison, but it was probably all bollix and sure money was fuck-all use to him, because he got killed in a car crash a few weeks after they let him out. I saw a good few people in The Joy try to get compo out of the prison by doing all kinds of things to themselves, but none of us who watched Slasher lose his finger that day were ever tempted to try it ourselves.

♦   ♦   ♦

A Decision

I've made up me mind. When I get out of here, I'm gonna put me name down for treatment. I know I'll always be a junkie. But I'm going to swap me heroin dependency for a physeptone one, swap a socially-unacceptable addiction for one which the Government will actually pay for. Get me bottle of phy every week for the rest of me life, however long that is. Sound as a pound. I'll live out me days in the same fuckin futile state that I have since I started on the gear. But legally.

♦ ♦ ♦

Merry Christmas (War is Over)

I'm woken by the sound of me door flinging open. "Merry Christmas!" the screw shouts at me. "Come on, up for your wash, make your bed and slop out as usual."

I can hear similar festive greetings echoing up and down the landings outside and, in between, the groaning of men who see no reason to get up and feel no urge to be anything but their usual cranky selves this morning, Christmas or no Christmas. "We've fuck-all to get up for," quite a few of the lads are shouting, along with, "Why can't we just stay in the scratcher all day?"

The mood's no better in the breakfast queue.

The screw checks that me and Redser are back in our peter, locks the door after us and tells us it'll be opened again in a couple of hours or so. Which is sound enough, because it gives us time to roll up a few joints. The block of hash I got in a few days ago should see the two of us through the Christmas. I share me stuff with Redser, because the poor bloke doesn't have nothing. His ma and da are dead and he doesn't have money or any friends who'd bring him in an'thin. I can't very well leave him there sitting out on his own like a Toblerone while I'm buzzin, can I? I pull out me skins and we roll about ten.

I think the mood has lightened considerably now, because all I can hear next door is fits of giggles, so the other lads must be up to the same thing as us. Blow has a strange effect on me. Sometimes I think I'm better off on the smack. Smack gives me that orgasmic rush and I'm nice to every fucker I meet until me body starts to crave it again. Blow's different. When the giggles stop, I turn into a right paranoid cunt, picking arguments with people for stupid reasons or no reason at all. It's after a few joints, when I start to feel all pissed off at the state Redser has the cell in – the messy cunt – that I suggest inviting someone else around to ease the tension, for dinner, like. "What about Tommy?" I ask.

Tommy is a steamer, though that's not strictly true, because he swings both ways. When I found out about this, I nearly fell off me fuckin bed. Not homophobia or an'thin. Like everyone else, I just thought he was the most screamingly heterosexual bloke in the whole gaff. He always had beautiful-looking birds in to see him and spent half his visits wearing the face off them. Fuckin rides, they were, every last one of them. I spent so much time staring at Tommy's visitors that I got to know them better than I did me own family. So when I found out that he liked men, it came as more than a bit of a shock. It seemed to be out of character. Then again, so did his reason for being in here in the first place. Killed a bloke, he did, in some row or other. Anyhow, me and Redser decide that he'd make a perfect dinner guest because we could slag him about being a steamer and take the piss out of that posh accent of his.

I bang on me door and call one of the screws, Flanno it is, to let me out for a slash. Flanno's a bollix. There's a general I-am-the-law attitude that surrounds the cunt and everything he does. It's important then, when I'm inviting Tommy over, that I tell him who's patrolling the landing in case he gets his gear lifted. On the way back from the jacks, I let a roar over to him. "Tommy, if you're bored, then head over to us for your dinner. We're having a bit of a chat, Christmas Day and all that."

"It would be a joy to," he shouts back, posh cunt.

"All right, just tell *Flanno* here and he'll let you over to us when you've got your tray, right?"

I don't think we've ever been so excited about the arrival of dinnertime in here. A whole morning on the auld blow has left us Hank Marvin, even for the shite they serve as food in here. Everyone has the munchies. As usual, me own hunger is in direct proportion to the number of cunts standing ahead of me in the queue and I think I'll never reach Raymo, who's wearing a paper tissue crown on top of his chef's hat. I just about make it before me legs give way.

"Would you like a starter?" he asks me.

"A what?"

"A starter."

"A starter? Are ye sure?"

"Yeh."

"Well, what is it?"

"Soup," he says, as though it's some exotic dish I'd never heard of before. Every other day of the year, a bowl of soup is called a bowl of soup in here. It's obvious that an effort is being made to make us feel like we're in some fuckin swanky restaurant for Christmas dinner and not a prison canteen, but they blow the effect they're aiming for straight away, because the soup is fuckin tomato and goes with fuck

164

all else in the dinner. Doesn't matter though, because like everyone else, I've held the bowl up to me mouth and milled it back before I get in smelling distance of the main course. I'm so hungry I wouldn't have had the strength to go on otherwise. Kenner, who's doing the meat, is just as smarmy as Raymo. "Choice of meats, sir," he says.

I stare at him. "What have ye got?"

"Turkey and ham, sir."

"Well, I don't fancy the turkey, it looks a bit too dry."

"No, it is not," he says, like it was a personal insult to him. "I cooked it myself."

"Ye did in your shite. They come in ready cooked. You only chopped the onions and shoved them up its arse." That's fucked him up. I go for checkmate now. "I just can't decide what to have. Is it possible to have turkey and ham?" I ask.

"Of course, it is, sir." He slaps a bit of each on me plate.

I reach the vegetable counter. "What have ye got?" I ask wearily.

"The finest fresh parsnips and turnips, chopped and marinated in a luscious sauce."

Luscious sauce, me arse. Fuckin gravy.

Have aliens taken over The Joy and turned everyone into bleedin robots or something? I'd prefer the like-it-or-fuckin-lump-it service we get 364 days a year to be honest. As I collect me jelly and ice-cream, I'm told, "There's a little surprise for you as well" and I'm handed a plastic cup of orange. Surprises don't come as little as that. I trudge off back to me cell with me tray.

By the time afternoon rec comes around, we're all either too stuffed, too drunk or too stoned to do anything as strenuous as playing snooker or table tennis, so we all sit outside our cells, our backs against the wall, smoking away. Perhaps it was from listening to Tommy during dinner, but suddenly I'm earwigging other conversations, listening to people's accents. It's difficult to know, sometimes, where the fuck half the people in this place are from. Lads from Blackrock, Bray and Baldoyle might not be real culchies, but they don't talk like Dubs, so to me they might as well be. Don't know where that fuckin Dublin 4 accent comes from, but it seems to be spoken all over Dublin these days. Like a bird I know from the estate. She moved up to the Navan Road a couple of year ago and now I need a fucking interpreter to talk to her.

Tea tonight is the usual pot of scald, no fuckin Christmas pudding or Christmas cake. One of the screws says yes when we ask whether Tommy can bring his mattress over and stay the night.

After lights out we smoke some more joints and the jokes become funnier and funnier to us and we giggle our way through the night. Every time Tommy opens his mouth, he has us in knots. "I really don't understand what you're laughing at," he says. Queen's English he talks. Queen's. Ha ha ha.

Nothing is out of order now. Anything goes tonight. So me and Redser start asking him about being a steamer. "Are ye more into women or men?" Redser says.

"Well, it depends who the women and men are, really," he says. "I wouldn't fancy either of you two for starters."

"Why not?" I ask, insulted, like.

"Because you're both extremely ugly."

That fucks us up.

"Can I ask you a straight question?" I say, not really caring whether he says yes or no. But he says yes. "What's it like to take that out and stick it up another bloke's arse?"

Redser breaks his balls laughing. Tommy cringes with disgust. "Don't be vulgar. That's absolutely frightful talk."

Then he starts giggling with us. He tells us then what it's like to have gay sex, what it's like to be bisexual and what it's like to walk into a nightclub and know that you could fancy anyone in the place, man or woman. Funny, it doesn't make me feel uncomfortable, dunno about Redser. Before today, we would both have said that, come the revolution, the steamers in this place would be up against the wall and shot along with the grasses and the rapists. Tonight, we're letting one sleep in our cell. Who says that blow doesn't expand your mind?

"Merry Christmas, lads," I say, dropping off.

The two boys giggle for the last time and then say it too. "Merry Christmas."

◆ ◆ ◆

MAKE YOUR VERY OWN SYRINGE

Enjoy hours of mindless fun with this easy-to-make syringe, which will allow you to shoot up in the privacy of your own cell.

You will need:

1. An uppity cunt of a screw who has just searched your peter and confiscated your works.

2. A ball-point pen.

3. Some matches.

4. A craving for heroin so bad you'd kill your granny if she tried to stop you getting the fuckin stuff into you.

5. Some sticky tape.

6. A needle.

7. Some heroin, ready cooked.

Method: Take the pen and dismantle it until you're left with just an open-ended plastic tube. Take a needle and tape it to the thin end, wrapping several layers of tape around it to ensure it's air-tight. As delicately as your shivering hands will allow, pour some of the ready-cooked heroin from your spoon into the other end. Lay out another piece of tape on the table, sticky side up, and put three matches down end to end on it. Wrap the tape around them and then push the whole thing into the tube until some of the heroin comes out of the needle tip. Now stick it into your arm.

This easy-to-make syringe can be used not only in conjunction with heroin, but also a wide range of other opium-based, pain-killing, intravenously-taken substances that act on the body's nervous system, including morphine, diconal, physeptone, palfium, pethidine, codeine and tamgesic. All are subject to availability. See your local dealer for details.

NB: Remember, the easy-to-make syringe has one draw-back. That is, it has no draw-back. It isn't possible to suck blood into the tube of the pen to make sure you've hit a vein, so you have to be sure. You might even like to get an adult to help you. Happy shooting!

◆   ◆   ◆

NOBODY LOVES YOU
WHEN YOU'RE DOWN AND OUT

Someone's dead. None of us knows who yet, but the word is all over The Joy. Joey, a shoplifter and car thief extraordinaire, came in about twenty minutes ago after getting a nine-month stretch and he saw the ambulance in the carpark. They were putting a covered body in the back, he said.

After a few hours spent confined to our cells, our imaginations are working overtime. All of us have several people that we hope it is. Overdose, suicide, I don't care, there are quite a few fuckers in here I'd like to see dead and I hope to meself that whoever it is, he is one off my list.

As we're let out to collect our lunch, we find out. There's something fuckin appropriate in the fact that it's the Hulk who breaks the news to us. "He's dead," he's saying excitedly. "The little faggot's dead."

"Who?" we say.

"Boyo. Hanged himself last night," he says, delighted with himself. "Little queer couldn't take it, eh?"

He was driven to it. Deep down, those of us who watched the things they did to him over the years and said nothin, we know we're as responsible as those who used to beat him, just for the heck of it. I've never seen the Hulk so happy. He's cracking jokes about him now. The Hulk, rapist himself and fuckin proud of it too, is typical of the fucked-up values at play in this shit-hole. Thank fuck I've only got a few months left of me sentence. I start to wonder how I'd cope if I was facing fifteen or twenty years in this nuthouse, whether like Boyo, I'd string meself up instead of trying to cope with it.

But why should I shed tears for Boyo. I think about what he did to those old ladies. And the young fellas he buggered as well. I can't shed any tears for someone like that, so I join everyone in laughing at the Hulk's latest joke about him. But then we hear, it's not Boyo at all. Just some other poor fuck, that no-one gives a shite about. By the time we've collected our lunch, we've forgotten all about him. We start to talk about the football. Villa lost last night. Again.

◆   ◆   ◆

RUNNING TO STAND STILL

This is me last-ever shot. How many times have I said that before? Fuckin plenty. Me hands are trembling. It's been how long since my last shot? Not long at all. But still too long.

I have a brand new spoon, which I managed to rob from the kitchen, right from under the screw's nose. I squirt some water onto it and pour the contents of the bag onto it as well. I stir it up and it's not long before it's bubbling hot. I drop the bit of filter in and it soaks up all the liquid. I press the works down on it and draw it in before attaching the needle. I sit on the floor, me back against the wall. I look at the works. The liquid inside it.

You're brown, you're beautiful and I love you. You make me feel so good. You make me feel like I'm good. Like I'm worth spending a bit of time with. You've always got time for me. You make me feel so ... worthwhile. Interesting. Humorous. Intelligent. Talented. Not vermin. A hero. Yeh, like a fuckin hero ... Sure, that's how you got your name, isn't it?

I'm running out of veins fast and I'm getting closer and closer to me auld crotch and the day when I'll have to inject into me prick. No, I think I'll probably die before then. Bad thought. Bad thought. Lose that thought. No better man. I stick the point of the needle against a throbbing vein at the top of me right leg, push it in, pull back and slam the stuff into me.

Interesting. Humorous. Intelligent. Talented. And ... Ah ... Oh ... Ah ... Sexual ... Yeh, sexual ...

Please don't ever leave me.

◆ ◆ ◆

MELLOW AND YELLOW

I can't believe what I saw on me way down to the jacks this morning. It happened right in front of all of us. Emptying your piss-pot underneath some culchie's door is bad enough, but Alkie whipped out his cock on the landing and just slashed in to the cell of that new fella from Cork, with everyone else walking past, like. If he'd been caught for that, he'd have lost his remission and everything but even at that hour of the morning he seemed to be too buckled to know what he was doing.

Redser's nearly pissing himself he thinks it's so funny. The buzz is good. We're smoking ourselves stupid this afternoon. I'm after getting in a block of hash yesterday. Usually I'm not really that into the blow. I've never cared much for recreational drugs at all, in fact. On the outside, I'd smoke it if there was a few of us sitting around listening to a bit of Bob Marley, which is fuckin corny, I know. I used to sometimes have a couple of joints after a turn-on, to bring me down like. But since that maintenance programme the judge made me go on last time I was out, me status has changed from strung-out junkie, who'd inject cat's piss into his veins if he thought he'd get a hit off it, to casual user who needs the occasional drug, even if it is only blow, to help him forget how fucked-up his life is.

We're lying in our cell, me and Redser, when he starts remembering his first night in the borstal. "Asleep I was, and someone in the cell above was shouting down to me. Out his window. I went over to me window and asked him what he wanted. He said he'd heard I was new in the place and he said I was very welcome."

"Did he?"

"Yeh. Said if I needed anything or if I was in any trouble or that, just to give him an auld shout like. Then he asked me whether I fancied a bit of Swiss roll."

"What time was this at?"

"About three in the fuckin morning ... I said yeh, you know, 'cos I didn't want to hurt his feelings. His ma had probably made it special or something. So I said yeh and he told me to hold me tray out the window and he'd drop it down and I could catch it. So that's what I did. Stuck it out the window and waited. He shouted down that it was coming. Then it hit the tray. *Wallop*. It wasn't Swiss roll."

"What was it?"

"Shite. It was a big fuckin lump of shite ... I started screaming and when I stopped all I could hear was laughing coming from all the cells around me."

I start breaking me bollix laughing as well. I light up another joint.

"So," he says, "what about you? What's your first memory?"

"Ah now, Redser, I remember everything about me very first day. From the court right up to the borstal. I was really strung out on the gear at the time and they got me over a load of cars and gaffs I did. Went down for the lot. Me brief told me I was gonna do time, but you still shite yourself when the judge says it, don't you? The judge just looked at me and said: 'You have been convicted of charges of larceny and robbery with violence. I see from your records that you have a problem with drug addiction, for which you have received treatment in the past. But it's a short, sharp shock you need.'"

Redser's laughing his arse off at me impression of the judge, who is a new addition to me repertoire, so I carry on. "'I am satisfied that only a custodial sentence will help to teach you the error of your ways. I am therefore sentencing you to six months' imprisonment in St Patrick's Institution.'"

I hand the joint over to Redser for a blast.

"So what happened then?" he asks.

"He looked at the pigs and then back at me and told them to take me down. They brought me downstairs to the cells under the court, where there were all these other young fellas waiting for their cases to come up. Typical lads, doing their best to put on the macho front, but beneath the surface they were like me, shiteing cunts who just wanted to be let go home ... So anyhow, I was put in this cell and had to stay there until they had a few more bodies to bring up to the borstal. All the other lads were asking me what I got, not out of concern or sympathy or an'thin, but just to suss out what kind of mood the judge was in. I remember some young lad telling me that six months was fuck-all. I'd do it on me piss-pot, he said. He didn't look old enough to know what he was talking about. Every time one of the young lads was called out, we'd all wish him luck and then we'd be betting with each other how long he'd get. Some of them were brought back down. Some weren't. Must have got suspended sentences ...

"Then they brought me up to this desk and there was this pig there eating a boiled egg sandwich. He asked me for me name and me address and a few other fuckin questions and started filling it all in on this form. The fuckin smell of his fuckin sandwiches was making me feel like puking all over his desk."

Me guts heave as I think about what happened next. When he asked me to "pour out the contents of your pockets, please," a lump of hard egg yolk, drippin in the fucker's spit, shot out of his mouth like a Polaris missile and landed on me cheek.

"Did ye wipe it off?" asked Redser.

"No, I left it there."

"Why the fuck?"

"I dunno. Maybe I didn't want to embarrass the cunt. That's fuckin stupid, isn't it? He's filling out the form to get me put away and I'm worried about his feelings ... Anyhow, he asked me again to empty out me pockets and I pulled out me smokes, me lighter, me keys and a couple of quid in loose change. But all the time I'm doing this, I'm working all the bleedin muscles in me face, trying to dislodge the piece of egg. It wouldn't budge though. I could feel it. There. Fuckin huge, it felt. It felt like it was burrowing its way into me face as well. Then he said I could keep me smokes, but not me lighter. And then he told me to hand over me watch and me ring. Then he just smiles at me, with his mouth open, and I thought I was definitely going to puke when I saw all that mashed-up egg and bread inside."

"Fuck's sake."

"So then he asks me to take off me belt and shoelaces. 'Just in case you're feeling suicidal,' he said, the smart bollix. I was gonna say I won't be once I wash half your fuckin lunch off me face, but I never said nothing. When they brought me off again, I just wiped it off with me sleeve."

"Then they brought you off in the van."

"Yeh, herded us all out into it like cattle being brought off to market. A few of the lads in the back were puking their rings up."

"Probably just after being interviewed by Egg Sandwich."

I laugh. "Nah, they were just shiteing themselves. There was eleven of us in the back altogether. Ten blokes and a bird."

"A bird?"

"Yeh, she was a prostitute. She had some neck. We were slagging her off like, but she was well able for us. One of the lads asked her how much it was for a blow job. She said it would be extra for him, because she'd have to spend hours looking for his prick. Another lad asked her was there any chance of a freebie and she just pointed at the first fella and said, 'Ask your friend, he hasn't got much to spend.' No-one slagged her after that. Then suddenly, we were there. The van stopped for ages and we heard these gates being opened. That's when I started getting the butterflies. We got out and I looked around me. The height of the wall. The watch towers. The razor wire. The pig shouted at us like a fuckin army major, 'Okay, sort yourselves out. Different lines, please. Mountjoy, St Pat's, female prison. Sort yourselves out, males, females and any other gender.'"

"Were you scared?"

"We all were. Well, all except–"

"The prostitute?"

I nod.

"What was she doing?"

"She was telling the pig that he could do anything he wanted for fifty quid and she'd even let his wife watch."

"So what happened?"

"Nothin. She got no business that night."

We both break our shites laughing. Redser hands the joint over to me. "Good days," he says. I agree. But that's the last of the hash. I've smoked the joint right down to the point where it's not going to be possible to hold it without burning me fingers. Soon we won't be laughing any more.

◆　　◆　　◆

A NEW LEAF

It was simple things I'd missed about home when I was in the slammer. I started to think about this as I was sitting at the kitchen table catching up on the football results and me ma was pottering around the place with her duster, singing tunelessly to herself. I looked up from me paper and just listened. I could just about make out the song. It was "The Candy Store on the Corner". Then a voice came out of the sitting room. I don't even remember whose it was. "Shut up that singing, will ye?"

I just went fuckin spare. "This is me ma's home. She can sing if she wants to, right? She can do what she likes. She's my mother. And she lives *here*."

She had to sit down and put her arm around me to calm me down. I just went mental. It was a rage born out of years of being told what to do and what not to do. There was that and then there was a lifetime's guilt, which was being amplified a thousand times by me ma's and da's kindness towards me since I got out of The Joy. For most of me thirty years, I have been a very, very bad son to them, but they always came to visit me and when I got out last year, they told me that their home would always be my home too, whether or not I made good me promise to stay off the gear.

As it happens, I haven't done badly at all. The physeptone keeps the aches and the psychosis away and, though all I've done is swap one addiction for another, I don't need to rob any more, which is just as well because I don't have the energy to run away from cops and shop security guards these days.

Life is ... Well, to be honest, life is shite. Boring, dull, pointless. Me average week seems to consist of nothing but standing in queues. Queue for me dole. Queue for me phy. Queue for me treatment up the hospital.

I've arrived at the conclusion that, after ten years on the gear, everything in life is shite, boring, dull and pointless. It's one great anticlimax from here on in. I could easily make what's left of it tolerable again by going back on the gear, but I'm not going to. I did have one little relapse at Christmas, when I went out and managed to get some uncut Colombian brown, at least, they said it was uncut. The one last shot us junkies always bullshit on about. Old habits and all that.

Maybe it was just that the experience of being inside at Christmastime has left a mark on me. That's why I had to have that hit on Christmas night. No, that's a load of bollix. I could think of a million reasons to explain why I took it, a million ways of rationalising my decision to start taking gear in the first place, none of which would even come close to the truth. Because I don't know what the truth is any more. It means fuck-all to you when you're a junkie, it becomes redundant. Heroin changes the whole way you see things. With heroin, Duffo used to tell me, you discover there is no such thing as the truth. It's only when you're on the gear that you can see that nothin is right and nothin is wrong. Everything is just a means to an end. I can't remember what we were doing when he was telling me this, either we were bombed out of it or it was just after we'd done over some poor cunt to get money to buy smack. He liked to rationalise things.

Sometimes I think Duffo would never have touched the gear if he had met this religious drug counsellor who tried to get me off it when I was about twenty-one. Duffo always thought too much and I think this guy would have gotten inside his head. He said that users experience not only a physical and mental deterioration, but a moral one too. You lose sight of truth and justice and the light of God, he told me. I think this guy was trying to colonise me fuckin soul for the Catholic church. Fuck all that, I told him at the time. It was bollix. Only reason I experienced a moral deterioration was because the stuff was illegal and therefore fuckin expensive and I had to go out and rob to pay for it on the black market. Had fuck-all to do with me actual use of the drug.

The Joy has scarred me for life. Some of the sick cunts who played cameo roles in me life inside now play lead roles in me nightmares. A recurring one has me as a seagull, trying to persuade Mad Frankie to let go of the lump of butter he's dangling from his window on a piece of twine. In another, the Hulk is beating me unconscious and trying to hang me.

But in a way I miss the place. You can't spend almost all of your adult life in an institution without feeling that you're somehow part of it or it's part of you. You can't lock a guy up for most of his life, tell him what time to get up, what time to exercise, what time to work, what time to read, what time to watch television, what time to play snooker, what time to shit, what time to go to bed; then open the doors one day and tell him to go out and start making decisions for himself. Me whole body clock is still set on Mountjoy time and I am obsessive in me habits. I get up early and go to bed early, eat me breakfast, dinner and lunch at the same times I did when I was inside. All because I haven't developed the ability to say, "Fuck it, I'll go out to the pictures at four o'clock and have me dinner at seven or half seven for a change."

So while me experiences in The Joy will never leave me, the place also represents security, a shelter, a sanctuary from the outside world. I don't ever want to live there again, but sometimes the urge to go back is overwhelming. There are days when I go up there and stand around outside for hours, for no reason other than – well, just to be *there*. Last week, I tried to get in to see Redser, so I could get inside the place and see what it's like again. They don't like ex-prisoners coming back to talk to their mates, so I pretended I was his brother, but they sussed me and kicked me out.

Redser's serving out the last couple of years of his sentence for a robbery he did. Like me, he's got the virus and he's talking about getting himself off the gear once he gets out. He told me in his last letter that I'm going to be his role model, which embarrasses me a bit. Most of the other lads I knew inside are either dead or dying or trying to keep one step ahead of the Gardaí.

Yeh, the Gardaí. That's probably the first time I've ever called them that. Tell you why. Last Thursday, I was walking down by Christ Church when four of them pulled up alongside me in a squad car. I thought they were just gonna hassle me or lift me and bring me in for questioning about something they already knew that I knew fuck-all about. So I didn't look at them, just carried on walking as they stopped the car just ahead of me and wound down the window. One of them, an auld cunt with whom I'd shared many late night question-and-answer sessions down the local station, stuck his head out and called me. By me nickname. I just stopped dead in me tracks. "Come here," he said.

I walked up to the car.

"How're you keeping?" he asked.

"Not bad," I said.

"How's the maintenance going?"

"Good."

"Off the gear?"

"Yeh. Miss it, but. Have to say it."

He nodded knowingly. "Total cure is just about impossible. That's what they say, isn't it?"

"Yeh."

"Well listen, you hang on in there, man. We're all rooting for you."

For a minute, I felt like a little kid. I thought he was going to put his hand through the window, toss me hair and call me "a little rascal".

"If you need anything at all, you know where we are," he said.

All I could think to do was nod me head.

The other three wished me luck and they drove off, leaving me just standing there in shock. I started to cry. Little tears first. Then floods. It was the first time someone in authority had ever made me feel like he really knew how I felt. It was like he was saying, "The old you is back. No hard feelings, right?"

I wish I'd said that to him. But if he reads this, I want him to know that there are none. No hard feelings at all.

◆   ◆   ◆

QUE SERA, SERA

The craving for a turn-on is there all the time, especially when I start to think that soon I'm going to die. The days are long and empty. The only things I have to get up for now are visits to the hospital, visits to the clinic, visits to the dole office, visits to local schools to lecture children about the error of my ways and walks down town to buy the cheap tobacco on O'Connell Bridge. How do I fit it all in, you might ask.

Then there are days like today, when I'm lying in hospital, under strict observation as the virus starts to take hold of me. Once I get a sniffle, they bring me in for a couple of weeks and pump me full of stuff to build up me strength again. I don't even ask what they're putting into me. Sure, I never asked questions when I was putting stuff into meself, so it makes no odds. It looks like I'm going to be in here for Christmas and New Year, which is upsetting me a bit because I don't think I've many of either left.

Me ma came in this morning, though, and we cheered each other up. She told me that one thing that had really improved about the flat since I came back was meal-times. When I got out of The Joy, I asked everyone at home could we all sit down together for dinner, as a family, just for one hour of every day. Usually, most of us either missed the meal completely or ate it standing up at the sink. So we were like a bunch of strangers all living in the same house. Sitting in a cell, eating off a tray, next to a bloke you don't know or don't like, teaches you just how precious families are. Anyhow, ma says she's learned stuff about her kids she never knew before they all started sitting down together to eat.

I was flipping through the new Argos catalogue this morning and I asked her to pick up one of these nice collapsible stools they're selling. Only £6.99 they are.

"What do you want that for?" she asked.

"It's for you, ma. I'm not being morbid or an'thin, but when I go, you can bring it up to the cemetery and sit by me grave and have a chat with me."

She was a bit surprised. "Don't be stupid. You'll see me down, son. There's no point in you buying it for me, because you'll be the one getting the use out of it."

"Well, tell you what. We'll go halves on it then, £3.50 each. Right? Whichever of us lives longest, right?"

She just touched me hand and smiled at me. I know she'll be the one getting the use out of it.

I'm tired most of the time now, and in pain as well, but I never mention it. Some people who get the virus wallow in it and play on other people's sympathies. But why should I tell me ma that I hurt. It's *my* illness. I brought it all on meself. I didn't know you could get the virus from needles when I started on gear, but it wouldn't have mattered to me even if I had known. I chose heroin. I knew that dangers went with it. I didn't give a fuck. I'm not an innocent victim and once you learn to accept that, then you can overcome all the feelings of hatred, guilt, self-loathing that go with this illness.

Just as I'm thinking this, Garvo comes into the ward. I knew him quite well in The Joy, though it was always a bad idea to let him into your cell. He was a professional pickpocket and house-stripper and he'd clean your fuckin peter out right under your nose without you seeing a thing. He once took three posters off me wall and fecked me works and me smokes as well while I was looking straight at him. He has the virus like me and he knows he's only a matter of weeks away from the end. He looks terrible. "Enjoying life?" he asks me.

"When you've got the virus," I tell him, "you don't enjoy life, you handle it."

"Glad to see someone's handling it."

"You're not?"

"How the fuck can I handle the fact that I might not be here next year?"

"Have you got a granny?" I ask him.

"Yeh, I have."

"How old is she?"

"She's eighty-nine."

"So how do you think she copes?"

He squinted his eyes. "What are you talking about?"

"Garvo, she's going through exactly the same feelings as you. She knows that death is getting closer for her as well."

"She's had a life though."

"Bollix. Doesn't make it any easier. We had lives as well, don't forget. Bloody good ones. I can't deny that the best days of me life were on gear and neither can you. Heroin was – fuckin great, man. There's no use us sitting here, lying our arses off saying it's shite, it's a mug's game. We both know that if we could afford it, we'd probably still be out there now taking it."

He nods.

"So given your life over again and knowing that if you took heroin there was a chance that something like this would happen, would you still do it?" I ask him.

"S'pose so."

"No suppose about it. 'Course you would. And so would I. We made our choices and we have to live with them. The thing is, when I got out of The Joy, I decided I wasn't going to bring anyone else down with me. What did me ma and da do to deserve that or any of the shit I've given them? So why not give them something nice to remember me by."

"Jaysus, you sound like my counsellor."

I laugh at the idea of me sounding like a social worker. "Just my way of getting by, Garvo."

"Our lives haven't changed much, have they?" he says.

"How do you mean?"

"Well, prison and hospital. There's not much difference is there? You keep bumping into the same people. The same faces. Same auld routine."

I nod.

He smiles and winks at me. "*Que sera, sera,*" he says. It was always a favourite saying of his. Then he gets up and goes.

I think about what he said. About how little our lives have changed. That the few people I called mates in The Joy are now me mates in hospital. That everything in me life is still mapped out for me by someone else. And this is me prison now. Yeh, not much has changed. I look down to the floor and start laughing. I laugh and laugh and laugh until I can't stop. Garvo is after robbing me slippers.

◆   ◆   ◆

GLOSSARY

bacco – *tobacco*

barrel – *body of a syringe*

blag – *a robbery*

boot – *money*

bricking – *frightened*

bulling – *angry*

burn – *tobacco*

caravan – *cells where travellers are kept*

divvy it up – *share out*

do a legger – *make a run for it*

eppo – *a fit*

fouler – *bad mood*

four-by-twos – *screws, warders*

gear – *heroin*

gee-gees – *veterinary drugs*

gicking himself – *shiteing with fear*

Hank Marvin – *starving, hungry*

hooch – *prison brew*

kept sketch – *kept watch*

kickers – *prison officers trained to keep order*

jacks roll – *toilet paper*

jockeys – *rapists*

jocks – *underpants*

Jo Maxi – *taxi*

lagged – *arrested*

lay-on – *drugs on credit*

jumpover – *a shop robbery*

Margaret Thatcher – *bed*

Moby Dick – *sick*

moolah – *money*

The Mun – *Ballymun*

munchies – *hunger pangs*

Ned Kelly – *belly*

hot Rosy – *tea*

Old Bill – *the police*

on yer Sweeney – *on your own*

the pad – *padded cell*

palf – *Palfium*

pigs – *the police*

pony and trap – *crap*

cup of scald – *cup of tea*

scratcher – *bed*

screw – *warder*

shiteing – *scared*

spike – *needle*

sponds – *money*

steamer – *homosexual*

strip cell – *padded cell*

rhythm and blues – *shoes*

take a redner – *to blush*

throwing me ring up – *vomiting*

throwing the head – *losing one's temper*

tin-roofer – *a spoofer*

to touch for – *to steal*

turn-on – *a fix of heroin*

works – *syringe*

MORE **TRUE CRIME** FROM THE O'BRIEN PRESS

STAKEKNIFE
Britain's Secret Agents in Ireland
Greg Harkin and Martin Ingram

An explosive exposé of how British military intelligence really works – from the inside. The stories of two undercover agents: the man known as Stakeknife, Force Research Unit (FRU) agent and deputy head of the IRA's infamous 'Nutting Squad', the internal security force which tortured and killed suspected informers; and Brian Nelson, who also worked for the FRU, and aided loyalist terrorists and murderers in their bloody work.

DEATH IN DECEMBER
The Story of Sophie Toscan du Plantier
Michael Sheridan

On 23 December 1996, the body of Sophie Toscan du Plantier was discovered outside her remote holiday cottage in West Cork. The attack had been savage and merciless. The murder caused shockwaves in her native France and in the quiet Cork countryside that she had chosen as her retreat from her glamorous lifestyle in Paris. Despite an extensive investigation, the killer of Sophie is still at large … the file remains open. Updated with an account of the Ian Bailey libel case.

THE GENERAL
Godfather of Crime
Paul Williams

Now a major motion picture by John Boorman.

In a twenty-year career marked by obsessive secrecy, brutality and meticulous planning, Martin Cahill, aka The General, netted over £40 million. He was untouchable – until a bullet from an IRA hitman ended it all. A compelling read, this book reveals Cahill's bizarre personality and the activities of the *Tango Squad* – the special police unit that targetted him using tactics employed against the infamous Kray Gang.

GANGLAND
Paul Williams

A compelling, chilling read, *Gangland* gives the inside story on a dark and sinister world. Who are the families that form the Irish mafia? What have been their most daring exploits? How do they hide their activities from the authorities? Williams examines the way in which they have spread their net across the country and beyond, reaping huge profits which allow them to live the high life while bringing misery to others.

THE BLACK WIDOW
The Catherine Nevin Story
Niamh O'Connor

When Tom Nevin was brutally murdered in Jack White's Inn on the morning of 19 March 1996, none seemed as grief-stricken as his widow, Catherine. She stood by his graveside holding a single red rose – the classic symbol of lost love. Four years later, Catherine Nevin stood in the dock, accused of murdering her own husband. The trial kept the entire country enthralled, as every day more bizarre stories emerged: contract killers, money laundering, the IRA, sexual affairs, plastic surgery, contacts in high places. It had all the ingredients of a bestselling thriller, but this was real life, with a real victim.

CRACKING CRIME
Jim Donovan – Forensic Detective
Niamh O'Connor

A fascinating look at the ground-breaking work of Dr Jim Donovan and his forensics team. Dr Donovan outlines the development of this relatively new and intriguing science. He and his scientists have been instrumental in solving some of the country's most high-profile crimes, often using the tiniest clue – a fingernail, a spatter of blood, hairs – to crack the case. But success has come at a price: Dr Donovan was the victim of a car bomb planted by Martin Cahill. But he survived and continued to track down criminals using only the weapons of science.

OTHER BOOKS FROM PAUL HOWARD

HOSTAGE
Notorious Irish Kidnappings

In the late 1970s and early 1980s Ireland was hit by a spate of high-profile kidnappings, such as Lord and Lady Donoughmore; Ferenka chief Dr Tiede Herrema; supermarket heir Ben Dunne; and, bizarrely, the Aga Khan-owned Epsom Derby-winner *Shergar*. The kidnappings had one thing in common – they were all the work of paramilitary forces, carried out either as fundraising efforts or for use as leverage to force the release of IRA prisoners. *Hostage* sheds new light on the ransom demands, the ordeals of the hostages, and police efforts to rescue them.

The fascinating inside stories of Ireland's most famous abduction cases.

THE GAFFERS
Mick McCarthy, Roy Keane and the team they built

Examines the complex and explosive dynamic between the two men who brought the Irish team to the World Cup in 2002, but whose relationship could not endure to the final round. He talks to the players, the management team and the fans, and raises serious questions about the role of the FAI. This is the full story of the Irish team, their World Cup campaign and soccer's greatest controversy.

The No. 1 Bestselling
Ross O'Carroll-Kelly Series

ROSS O'CARROLL-KELLY, THE MISEDUCATION YEARS

The first book in the ROCK trilogy, introducing us to the suave and studly Ross on home ground: Castlerock Boys' School. Lord of all he surveys, from the ruggerbuggers to the rugger-huggers, Ross is in no hurry to quit school, and as long as he can keep repeating the Leaving Cert, there's no need to! This is where it all began: the formation of the phenomenon that is Ross O'Carroll-Kelly.

ROSS O'CARROLL-KELLY, THE TEENAGE DIRTBAG YEARS

So there I was, roysh, class legend, schools rugby legend, basically all-round legend, when someone decides you can't, like, sit the Leaving Cert four times. Well that put a focking spanner in the works. But joining the goys at college wasn't the mare I thought it would be, basically for, like, three major reasons: beer, women and more women. And for once I agree with Fionn about the, like, education possibilities. I mean, where else can you learn about Judge Judy, laminating fake IDs and, like, how to order a Ken and snog a girl at the same time? I may be beautiful, roysh, but I'm not stupid and this much I totally know: college focking rocks.

ROSS O'CARROLL-KELLY, THE ORANGE MOCHA-CHIP FRAPPUCCINO YEARS

So there I was, roysh, enjoying college life, college birds and, like, a major amount of socialising. Then, roysh, the old pair decide to mess everything up for me. And we're talking totally here. The next thing I know, roysh, I'm out on the streets. Another focking day in paradise for me! If it hadn't been for Oisinn's apartment in Killiney, the old man paying for my Golf GTI and JP's old man's job offer it would have been, like, a complete mare. But naturally, roysh, you can never be sure what life plans for you next. At least, it came as a complete focking surprise to me ...

ROSS O'CARROLL-KELLY, PS, I SCORED THE BRIDESMAIDS

So there I was, roysh, twenty-three years of age, still, like, gorgeous, living off my legend as a schools rugby player, scoring the birds, being the man, when all of a sudden, roysh, life becomes a total mare. I don't have a Betty Blue what's wrong, but I can't eat, I can't sleep. I don't even want to do the old beast with the two backs, which means a major problem and we're talking big time here. Normally my head is so full of, like, thoughts, but now I'm down to just one: Sorcha. I'm playing it Kool and the Gang, but this is basically scary. I mean, I'm Ross O'Carroll-Kelly for fock's sake, I don't *do* love.